12
*Lessons
to reach the
permanent the
memory.*

The SUNDAY SCHOOL
BOOK

Dave & "Putter" Weeks

Dave & "Putter" Weeks

The Sunday School Book (*TSSB*) is radical, but it is also realistic. It will bring every reader back to the true joy of learning. There is something deep down in the heart of every child of God that longs to know more about Jesus and His Word. If you look carefully, you will see that Jesus is pictured in every lesson. Learning more about Him and hiding His Word in your heart is the first step toward growth and being able to minister to others. Enjoy the journey!

12 Lessons to reach the permanent memory.

The SUNDAY SCHOOL BOOk

Dave & "Putter" Weeks

By

DAVE AND "PUTTER" WEEKS

© 2016

PUBLICATIONS

Baptist World Cult Evangelism
P.O. Box 836
Dacula, GA 30019-0014
www.bwce.org

All quotations of Scripture are taken from the Authorized King James Version.

THE SUNDAY SCHOOL BOOK

© 2016 Baptist World Cult Evangelism

P.O. Box 836, Dacula, GA 30019-0014

Printed by Facing the Facts, Dacula, GA

Cover by Addyman Design

Printed in the United States of America

Library of Congress Control Number: 2016902991

Weeks, Dave and "Putter"

The Sunday School Book / by Dave and "Putter" Weeks.

p.cm.

Includes an index and bibliographical references.

ISBN 978-1535258395 (Paperback)

1. CHURCH — SUNDAY SCHOOL LITERATURE. 2. TEXT BOOKS — EDUCATIONAL LITERATURE. 3. CATECHISM — INSTRUCTIONAL LITERATURE. 4. PEDAGOGY (CHRISTIAN).

FOREWORD

Long before this book was written or likely even conceived in the mind of its author, I watched him transform a Junior Boys Sunday School class into an effective learning center. As a member of that class, I not only watched what Dave Weeks did, I experienced it. That experience permanently changed my life. In fact, the change was so dramatic that, without it, I likely would not be in the ministry today.

I have never had a spiritual teacher who took his responsibility more seriously than Dave Weeks did. The Lord used him to point me in the right direction at an age in which I was still young enough to be molded yet old enough to be seriously directed.

Brother Weeks was not the only man God used in my life. My father and grandfather modeled before me the character they sought to instill in my life. My high school principal and several Christian school teachers were also great mentors.

My point, though, is that Sunday School teachers need to realize the incredible and eternal difference they can make in the lives of their students if they will take their teaching task seriously. Dave Weeks took that task very seriously, and I'm one of the students that was forever changed as a result.

Of course, God not only uses men. He uses women, too, and that certainly applies to Dave's wife, whom he affectionately calls "Putter." She has been a tremendous helpmeet to him for many years, and her performance of that role is also evident in her contribution to this book.

Whether you are a Sunday School teacher or student, you are holding in your hands a book that can make a profound impact on your life and the lives of others within your sphere of influence. I urge you to take it seriously and to devote the time and effort required to be a true learner yourself so that God may use you to be a true teacher of others (Ezra 7:10; 2 Tim. 2:15).

Kevin Callahan, President,
International Partnership Ministries
Phil. 3:13-14

PROLOGUE

Before you read any further, I would like to tell you a short story about what led me to the point of no return in committing to this publication. Having had several surgeries on my fingers, hands, and elbow, I became well acquainted with my orthopedic surgeon. We often discussed subjects of mutual interest. One day, he gave me a special prayer request concerning his upcoming recertification exam. He explained that, as a surgeon, he must be recertified every 10 years to retain his surgical license. The purpose of this examination is to demonstrate a continued competence (a working knowledge) as an orthopedic surgeon.

When I began thinking of people in my own profession (or calling) who deal with spiritual life-and-death situations almost every day, anxiety gripped my soul. Because the pressures on those in positions of spiritual leadership involve so many things outside the realm of *rightly dividing* [to cut straight or expound correctly] *the word of truth,* levels of continued competence (a working knowledge) in areas of doctrine, hermeneutics, and homiletics had dropped to an all-time low. Many leaders were no longer at the top of their game as compared to their not-so-distant past selves and peers. A general knowledge of what they believed was more prevalent among them than a working knowledge. They were no longer able to "get the car started," and people began to look elsewhere for abler "mechanics."

WORKING vs. GENERAL KNOWLEDGE

Spark plug wires must be connected to the engine
in their correct firing order, or the car will not start.

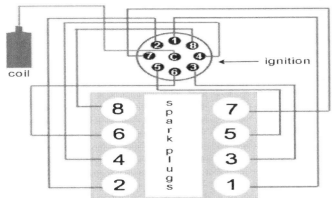

front of engine

A person with a working knowledge of this engine
knows where to connect the spark plug wires to the
ignition. A person with a general knowledge knows
only that the spark plug wires connect to the ignition.
He cannot get the engine to start.

When Christians have a working knowledge of Bible
doctrine, they will be equipped and ready to do the
work of the ministry effectively.

INTRODUCTION

The burden of writing *TSSB* . . . where did it all begin? It began nearly 20 years ago. I was asked to teach a 50s class in the absence of their regular teacher. Many of these people had been in Sunday school for over 25 years. I began by asking how many had been born again. They all raised their hands. Then the question was asked, "Who can say what it means to be born again?" Several hands went up. After listening to about four of them, it was obvious that not one of them had a clue as to what the phrase truly meant (to be born from above or born of God—having a spiritual birth; John 3:3-7). This prompted me to ask more questions, but the results were the same. At that point, it was apparent that whatever they had learned in Sunday school over the previous 25 years had not reached their permanent memory, and they had no Biblical foundation. They were unequipped to do the work of the ministry. Ways to correct this problem and create learning centers are the heart and soul of this book. You can be the first to get it started.

One of the first questions asked by those who recognize the need to change their approach is, "How do I make the transition from a speaker to a teacher?" Here are some helpful suggestions on where to begin.

Knowing the difference between speaking and teaching is the first step in making the transition. A lecturer or speaker does just that: lectures or speaks. The listeners hear but often do not apply—or even remember—what they have heard. In contrast, a teacher teaches so that students learn and apply knowledge until that knowledge becomes part of their memories. Although this concept is not foreign to the school classroom, our Sunday school classes have often become places for speakers or lecturers/listeners rather than learning centers for teachers/students. To make the transition and help students commit Biblical principles to permanent memory, class leaders must first shift their thinking and consider ways to teach that include more student participation and application of knowledge. One way is to use quick learners to help and teach other class members.

First, creating a learning center may require that the instructor start a new class called The Learners Class (depending on the age and willingness of the class members) because some people may not be interested in learning. Such a radical change may not be appealing to them after spending so many years just being listeners. The Learners Class must be voluntary. Some people are looking only for social connections and not a learning environment. The combination of a class leader who really wants to teach and students who really want to learn is what makes a difference. This transition will renew something deep inside of every saved person's soul, something that stems from the desire to develop and strengthen his or her relationship with the One who is the Redeemer, Savior, and Lord.

Next, the class will work together as a team to help one another through the entire process of memorization, recitation, and continuation. As soon as one person in the class has memorized the lesson content or a section of the lesson content, he or she will immediately begin to assist the others (help the teacher) in doing the same until all class members have memorized the material. Continued application is what drives this information deeper and deeper until it reaches the permanent memory.

In addition, what one has memorized must be understood based on its context. For example, in Lesson 1, what was God's purpose for giving the Ten Commandments? As the Scripture tells us, *Wherefore the law* [a reference to the Ten Commandments] *was our schoolmaster to bring us unto Christ, that we might be justified by faith* (Galatians 3:24). This helps develop the ultimate goal of hermeneutical correctness in knowing how to rightly divide the

Word of truth and incorporate it into the experiences of everyday life.

All teachers who produce such an outcome will be called "blessed" by all of their students. Revival, renewal, and rejoicing will be the natural results, and people will then have the missing part of their Christian experience that they have so longed for but never found.

One of the main reasons that cults are boasting that many of their converts are ex-Baptists (especially Jehovah's Witnesses) is that the converts said they had never learned anything in Sunday school. To try to do something that would help turn this situation around, I published *Back To Basics* in 1997. Although it became the most popular item on my book table, it did very little to resolve the problem. The problem was and is that people in our Sunday school classes were not learning because they were not being taught. When I was in Bible college, I clearly remember having two different kinds of teachers—one who told me things that he had never learned himself and another who taught me things that he had learned and retained in his permanent memory. Can you imagine a second-grade teacher having to look at her three-ringed notebook to teach the times table of twos? This is exactly what has destroyed the foundations of our Sunday school classes all across this land.

So what is the solution to the problem? When I came across this Scripture in Psalms, I knew precisely what the answer was.

Psalms 11:3

3 If the foundations be destroyed, what can the righteous do?

The answer is that the righteous must do what they have always done: **rebuild the foundations**!

TSSB takes us back to the rudiments of what learning is and how to do it. Memorization is only the first step in the learning process. One memorizes the times tables before one is given a complex reading problem that requires one to apply what one has learned. In Proverbs 1:7, the fear of the Lord is said to be the beginning of knowledge; after that comes understanding and wisdom. In the overview of the first lesson, "Putter" gives us some insights into how people learn differently and what is required in the first step of reaching the permanent memory. A desire to use knowledge in a Christ-honoring way will lead one to understanding and wisdom.

We are thrilled to be able to give you something that continues to affect the lives of all those who have the desire to be equipped for the work of the ministry. That something is learning things meant to reach the permanent memory with Biblical truths that will anchor the soul. The 12 lessons in *TSSB* do more than just equip learners; they safeguard them from becoming prey to false teachings. The first challenge introduced by false teachers is the Trinity. If someone were to ask you what the Trinity is or to explain it, what would you say? Before you try to answer that—what would you say if someone asked you what two times four is? Of course you would say eight. The reason that you can do that is that you had a teacher who reached your permanent memory with this information early on in grade school. Well, this same goal must become part of every Sunday school class, with an instructor who is a teacher and students who want to be learners. Where does the idea of reaching the permanent memory come from? It comes from Scripture. In the following three passages, the idea of having God's Word in one's heart is expressed plainly.

Psalms 119:11

<u>Thy word have I hid in mine heart</u>, that I might not sin against thee.

John 15:7

If ye abide in me, and <u>my words abide in you</u>, ye shall ask what ye will, and it shall be done unto you.

Colossians 3:16

Let the <u>word of Christ dwell in you richly</u> in all wisdom. . . .

"Hide," "abide," and "dwell" are all words that are used to reference the permanent memory. Memorizing God's Word as well as its context is the first step in building a foundation that will stay the course.

The typical Sunday school class has someone who is a speaker and people who are listeners. One profound educator and teacher, Dr. Bruce Wilkinson, emphasizes the importance of understanding this statement: "Speaking is not teaching, and listening is not learning." Our Sunday school classes need to be transformed from listening centers into learning centers. The time to start this transition is right now because people who really have an interest in learning God's Word are being attracted to learning centers that are teaching errors.

"Putter" and I have teamed up to make *TSSB* practical and effective. In Lesson 9, she has written the article called "Women in Leadership." Also, her introduction to the Section 1 Overview begins by giving the reader an understanding of how information is received by the brain and the different ways people learn. Knowing something about these differences can make learning a wonderful and rewarding experience for all your students. Once something is in the permanent memory, it stays. For example, your name and your birthdate are so deeply ingrained in your memory that normal, healthy people have instant recall of them. John 3:16 was the first verse that I learned in German. During my years as a missionary in Austria, it reached my permanent memory, and it's still there today. God made us this way, and we need to use what He has given us for His glory.

First of all, the 12 lessons in this book will transform speakers into teachers. Then, the teachers will see their students' minds filled with the wonders and awesomeness of their Creator. They will be empowered by the ability to use what they have learned to do the work of the ministry. Yes, all students will be able to answer the Trinity question as easily as if someone had just asked them their names. Let's give it a try. "Trinity," a word used to speak of the eternal relationship of the members of the Godhead—God the Father, God the Son, and God the Holy Spirit. Could you explain the Trinity? Yes, sure: it is the belief that God is one eternal being in three eternal persons. Thank you, sir! Just think of how Christians who have truths like this in their permanent memory could make a positive impact on a world that is in spiritual chaos. Do you want to be one of them? OK, let's get started!

How would you integrate *TSSB* into your Sunday morning and Wednesday night programs? First of all, because a learning center is so different from what people have been used to (especially after completing the young adult classes), it must be voluntary. You can't force people to learn if they don't have the desire to do so. The desire to become a teacher rather than a speaker will be acknowledged by one's willingness to memorize the content part of any or each of the 12 lessons in *TSSB* before one can assume the role of teacher. This is what makes a person eligible to stand before a class in a learning center as a teacher. When a lesson reaches the permanent memory, the learner is qualified to be certified for that lesson from the *www.tssbedu.net* website. When one has all 12 lessons in one's permanent memory, one can receive a *TSSB* certification. It is the mark of a worker who is equipped and ready to do the work of the ministry.

Because both the teachers' and the upper-class students' enrollment is voluntary, it eliminates the need to pressure class members to be diligent with their homework assignments, which consist of learning, teaching, and application.

It is our prayer that the Lord start a learning center in each one of His churches where the people have this desire. It would be called The Learners Class, and the 12 lessons in *TSSB* would be taught to equip each class member for the work of the ministry. When someone has memorized a lesson with the goal of having it reach the permanent memory, he or she will immediately become a teacher-helper in the class until every student has reached that threshold. The application part is a commitment to teach others what one has learned for the rest of his or her life.

SECTION 1: LESSONS FOR ALL

Lesson 1: The Ten Commandments

Lesson 2: The Triunity of God

Lesson 3: The Whole Armor of God

Lesson 4: The 10 Basic Doctrines

Section 1 Overview

A good place to start is 2 Timothy 2:15: "Study to show thyself approved unto God, a workman that needeth not to be ashamed, rightly dividing [to cut straight or expound correctly] the word of truth."

As Christians, we should take the words of Paul to Timothy seriously. To tell others what God's Word is saying, we must first know how to rightly divide it. We must know how to live by faith, defend the faith, and grow in faith. Failing to do this is what will make us ashamed. Also, we are told to be ready:

1 Peter 3:15

15 But sanctify the Lord God in your hearts: and be ready always to give an answer to every man that asketh you a reason of the hope that is in you with meekness and fear.

How do we do this? By getting Scripture into our permanent memory. Whatever we learn, our goal as students should be to get the information into our permanent memory. And as teachers, the goal is to get the information into our students' permanent memory.

There are numerous verses in Scripture that explain why it is so important to have instant recall of God's Word. Here are some of them:

Psalms 119:11
11 Thy word have I hid in mine heart, that I might not sin against thee.

When you hide the Word of God in your heart, it is in your permanent memory and can be recalled when needed.

John 15:7

7 If ye abide in me, and my words abide in you, ye shall ask what ye will, and it shall be done unto you.

To have Christ's words abiding in you is to have them in your permanent memory. Your memory will give you access to these words whenever they are needed.

Colossians 3:16

16 Let the word of Christ dwell in you richly in all wisdom; teaching and admonishing one another in psalms and hymns and spiritual songs, singing with grace in your hearts to the Lord.

When the Word of Christ dwells in you, it is in your permanent memory, and it can be used by the Holy Spirit and others to teach you. It replaces the natural impulses generated by your flesh. It's the way to victory.

The Teacher

What makes a good teacher? We have all had one or two teachers who stand out in our mind. As I am writing this, I am thinking of one of my 12th grade teachers, Mr. Hess. He was a good teacher, but what made him good? First, he treated all his students with respect. Second, he made class interesting and incorporated material for all three main types of learners into his lectures (we will get into the different ways students learn in the next chapter). Third, he convinced us that everything he was teaching us was something we needed to know, not only to receive a credit to graduate but also to know for life. And most important, he knew and experienced everything he was teaching us, and he enjoyed teaching. Yes, Mr. Hess was a good teacher, and 50 years after graduating, I am still amazed at how much I remember from his classes. He was right: I had a need to know everything he taught us.

Why take the time to tell you about my 12th grade Problems of Democracy and Economics teacher, Mr.

Hess? To introduce to you what separates a teacher from a good teacher. Mr. Hess was not teaching lessons; he was teaching students. There is a big difference. So many teachers study hard to teach a lesson, and when they walk into a classroom, that is what they do: they teach a lesson and not students. They content dump! All the research that they have done for the topic at hand is dumped on the students and buries them in information. The students have to sift out what is important and what they need.

It is the job of a teacher to make students learn. How is this done? There are three important tools to use in helping students learn:

1. Students must see the <u>need</u> to learn the subject at hand.

2. They must be held <u>accountable</u> for learning it. (In elementary school, do you think you would have learned to spell that list of vocabulary words if you didn't have a test on Friday?)

3. They must see an <u>application</u> for what they are learning.

When teaching principles and doctrines from the Bible, we see the need, the accountability, and the application as well as why it is important to get the material into the permanent memory.

Look at this again. 2 Timothy 2:15: "Study to show thyself approved unto God, a workman that needeth not to be ashamed, rightly dividing [to cut straight or expound correctly] the word of truth."

Matthew 28:19
19 Go ye therefore, and teach all nations, baptizing them in the name of the Father, and of the Son, and of the Holy Ghost:
20 Teaching them to observe all things whatsoever I have commanded you: and, lo, I am with you always, even unto the end of the world. Amen.

Who wants to be ashamed when standing before the Lord and give an account of why we did not know how or what to say to help someone? The application is to go and teach others.

The Student

To help your students learn, you must first understand your responsibility as a teacher. Yes, it is the teacher's responsibility to make the students learn, and to make them learn, we first must understand that not everyone learns in the same way.

Psalms 139:14
14 I will praise thee; for I am fearfully and wonderfully made: marvellous are thy works; and that my soul knoweth right well.

Not everyone learns in the same way, for we are fearfully and wonderfully made, even in the way we learn. As teachers, we need to be mindful of the different ways people learn and teach them according to their learning ability. We can incorporate the learning tools for our students into our lessons once we understand the three types of learning styles.

They are auditory, visual, and kinesthetic (tactile). Let's take a closer look at each of them and become familiar with how to identify the learning styles because they vary from student to student.

Auditory Learner

Auditory learners tend to learn best through traditional lecture-style teaching, in which information is given through the teacher's speaking. They are blessed with an incredible memory to recall what they have heard. They learn by repeating the information over and over until it is in their permanent memory. They also learn by word association; for example, by using acronyms or acrostics in music, they learn the notes on the spaces by remembering the word "face": F, A, C, E.

And they learn the notes on the lines E, G, B, D, and F by memorizing the sentence "Every good boy does fine." Auditory learners learn best when information is presented to and requested from them verbally.

Visual Learner

This type of learner does well with using visuals to learn something new. These learners benefit from diagrams, charts, pictures, and films as well as written instructions. They are the students who will need to write things down and take notes.

Kinesthetic (Tactile) Learner

This type of learner is a hands-on learner. These learners will learn best through physical activity in which they can touch, move, build, or draw what they are learning. They learn best when an activity goes along with the lesson.

Summary

The auditory learner learns by hearing. These learners understand and remember what they have heard and have an easier time understanding spoken instructions than written ones. One way to help auditory learners is to allow them to read out loud and use flash cards (read them out loud too). Encourage them to read their assignments out loud and record themselves so that they can hear the information. If possible, read questions on tests out loud for them.

The visual learner understands and remembers things by sight. These learners learn best by using methods that are primarily visual. Ways to help visual learners: use flash cards to learn new words and help them visualize the information by writing down key words, ideas, and instructions, and draw pictures to explain the information. Another learning aid would be to color-code the key words to help them remember new information.

The kinesthetic (tactile) learner learns by touching and doing. Physical movement is the key to these learners, who are hands-on. They often use their hands when speaking, so use that strategy to help them by using hand motions to teach new information. Flash cards can also help these learners, but remember that they learn best by doing—not just reading, seeing, or hearing.

The following is a link to a test to find out what type of learner you and/or your students are:

http://www.educationplanner.org/students/self-assessments/learning-styles-quiz.shtml

Section 1 Overview Memorization

Question 1: What is the goal of teaching?

Answer: The goal of teaching is to get the information into the students' permanent memory.

Question 2: What is the responsibility of the teacher?

Answer: The responsibility of the teacher is to make students learn.

Question 3: What are the different types of learners?

Answer: Three different types of learners are auditory, visual, and kinesthetic.

Question 4: What are the keys to learning and retention?

Answer:

A-Students must sense a need to learn.

B-They must be held accountable by teachers' testing them on the lesson content.

C-Students must use what they have learned in everyday life applications, thereby teaching others.

LESSON 1: THE TEN COMMANDMENTS

. . . *Sir, we would see Jesus.* Yes, you will find Him in the law, for Jesus is the law maker and the law keeper.

Why would learning the Ten Commandments be the number-one lesson? Why not? They were the first lesson that God taught the Israelites (Exodus 20). They were given by God and taught often by Jesus and the Apostle Paul. They teach the character and nature of a holy and righteous God and the fact that He alone should be worshipped and given honor above anything or anyone else in our lives. They are the moral standards He requires one to have with others. They are the very basics of the Christian faith wherever it is taught and are woven into our very own legal system. John Quincy Adams, the sixth president of the United States, said, "The law given from Sinai was a civil and municipal as well as a moral and religious code . . . laws essential to the existence of men in society and most of which have been enacted by every nation which ever professed any code of laws." On the Supreme Court building in Washington, D.C., Moses is etched carrying a tablet of the Law.

The Ten Commandments are a good starting point for teaching about obedience to God and parents and for teaching morality to new converts and children. Perhaps the most important reason to teach (learn) them is best expressed by Paul in Galatians 3:24: "Wherefore the law was our schoolmaster to bring us unto Christ, that we might be justified by faith."

How does the Law, the Ten Commandments, apply to us today? It applies in two ways. First, the Law is used to show people that they are lost and need Christ as their Savior. The Law also is a moral standard for saved people to follow. Once the Law has brought a lost person to Christ, his heart is changed and the Holy Spirit makes God's Law present in his heart and mind. How do we show a present-day application and need of the Law? The answer is found in Galatians and Hebrews:

Hebrews 10:16

This is the covenant that I will make with them after those days, saith the Lord, I will put my laws into their hearts, and in their minds will I write them.

Galatians 3:24–25

24 Wherefore the law [the moral law, the Ten Commandments] was our schoolmaster to bring us unto Christ, that we might be justified by faith.

25 But after that faith is come, we are no longer under a schoolmaster.

The schoolmaster is not the teacher but rather the one who brings the student to the teacher to learn. In Old Testament days, the schoolmaster was a slave whose job was to walk the child to the school and make sure he was brought to the teacher for instruction. The Ten

Commandments act like the schoolmaster in bringing us to Christ.

First, they reveal our sinful nature to us. The Apostle Paul says it best in Romans 7:7: "What shall we say then? Is the law sin? God forbid. Nay, I had not known sin, but by the law: for I had not known lust, except the law had said, Thou shalt not covet."

In the New Testament, the Ten Commandments are presented and serve as our schoolmaster who brings us unto Christ, who *is the end of the law for righteousness,* so that we might be justified by faith in Him.

Romans 10:4
4 For Christ is the end of the law for righteousness to every one that believeth.

How and why is Christ the end of the Law? He was the One who did not transgress any of the Law, for He was sinless, and He paid the final sacrifice for all mankind. He paid the penalty of the Law, which is death.

Hebrews 10:10

10 By the which will [In accordance with God's will] we are sanctified through the offering of the body of Jesus Christ once for all.

In the New Testament, Jesus brings all Ten Commandments down to only two:

Mark 12:29–31

29 And Jesus answered him, The first of all the commandments is, Hear, O Israel; The Lord our God is one Lord:

30 And thou shalt love the Lord thy God with all thy heart, and with all thy soul, and with all thy mind, and with all thy strength: this is the first commandment.

31 And the second is like, namely this, Thou shalt love thy neighbour as thyself. There is none other commandment greater than these.

In Romans, Paul has this to say about the Law:

Romans 13:8–10

8 Owe no man any thing, but to love one another: for he that loveth another hath fulfilled the law.

9 For this, Thou shalt not commit adultery, Thou shalt not kill, Thou shalt not steal, Thou shalt not bear false witness, Thou shalt not covet; and if there be any other commandment, it is briefly comprehended in this saying, namely, Thou shalt love thy neighbour as thyself.

10 Love worketh no ill to his neighbour: therefore love is the fulfilling of the law.

The Ten Commandments are reduced to two, and these two are of one principle: love. Love—first to the Lord and then to others. When we truly love the Lord with all our heart, mind, and soul and love our neighbors as ourselves, then we will follow the moral laws throughout our lives. But this is only possible through accepting Christ as our personal Lord and Savior, who was the only One able to fulfill the Law and keep all Ten Commandments.

Learning the Ten Commandments will also help us apply to our lives these three very important concepts of God: the righteousness of God and judgments of God, our social requirements toward other people, and how to conduct holy lives as children of God.

Once the Ten Commandments (God's Word) reveal sin and what it is to men, then can the Holy Spirit accomplish His convicting work in the heart.

John 16:8–9

8 And when he [the Holy Spirit] is come, he will reprove the world of sin, and of righteousness, and of judgment:

9 Of sin, because they believe not on me.

Titus 3:5

5 Not by works of righteousness which we have done,

but according to his mercy he saved us, by the washing of regeneration, and renewing of the Holy Ghost.

Ephesians 2:8–9

8 For by grace are ye saved through faith; and that not of yourselves: it is the gift of God.

9 Not of works, lest any man should boast.

We find the Ten Commandments listed in both Exodus 20:1–17 and Deuteronomy 5:6–21. They were given at Mount Sinai shortly after the Israelites came out of Egypt, around 50 days after their exodus. The first five have to do with the Israelites' relationship with the Lord, and the last five have to do with their relationship with their fellow men. They are listed here in a somewhat abbreviated form:

1. I am the LORD thy God. . . . Thou shalt have no other gods before me.

2. Thou shalt not make unto thee any graven image. Thou shalt not bow down thyself to them, nor serve them.

3. Thou shalt not take the name of the LORD thy God in vain.

4. Remember the Sabbath day, to keep it holy.

5. Honour thy father and thy mother.

6. Thou shalt not kill.

7. Thou shalt not commit adultery.

8. Thou shalt not steal.

9. Thou shalt not bear false witness [lie].

10. Thou shalt not covet.

Commandments Explained and New Testament Counterpart

First Commandment: I am the LORD thy God, Thou shalt have no other gods before me.

The first commandment demands an exclusive covenant with the LORD for our worship, love, praise, and service. Anytime we give anything or anyone else the praise and glory that is due to the Lord, we stand in danger of breaking this commandment—whether it be our own pride, our accomplishments and our status in life, or our possessions and our own families. He is to be our One and Only God. Here is a good question to ask yourself in regard to the first commandment: in my life, is the Lord present, prominent, or preeminent?

Verses from the New Testament:
Matthew 22:37
37 Jesus said unto him, Thou shalt love the Lord thy God with all thy heart, and with all thy soul, and with all thy mind.

Second Commandment: Make no images, Thou shalt not bow down thyself to them, nor serve them.

"Graven image" means a statue made of wood or stone, and "likeness" means a picture drawn on a wall or any flat surface such as paper. We are not to make, bow down to, or serve any idols. Idols become gods. Remember Exodus 32:8 and the golden calf?

Verse from the New Testament:
1 John 5:21
21 Little children, keep yourselves from idols. Amen.

Third Commandment: Thou shalt not take the name of the LORD thy God in vain; for the LORD will not hold him guiltless that taketh his name in vain.

The first thing that comes to mind when we read this commandment is cursing, swear words, and profanity. Yes, this is definitely a part of the commandment, and Christians should not use the Lord's name in this manner of speaking, but this also means we should not take or make the Lord's name common nor use it lightly, irreverently, or in a senseless manner. How often do we say His name without thinking of the Holiness behind it?

How often, when we are surprised or frightened, do we use His name? How often, even in our prayers, do we repeat His name over and over again until it has lost the value of who He is and what He does? There are also "minced oaths"; these are words that are substitutes for the Lord's name. How often do we use these? With today's lingo, we even use abbreviations when we text or are on Facebook; we need to be mindful of using these too.

This commandment is actually in two parts. The first is taking the name of the Lord in vain, and the second is what will happen when we do. We often do not think about the last part of the verse and commandment: the Lord will not hold him guiltless that takes His name in vain.

Verse from the New Testament:

51

Matthew 12:36

26 But I say unto you, That every idle word that men shall speak, they shall give account thereof in the day of judgment. (See also Colossians 3:8, Ephesians 5:4.)

Fourth Commandment: Remember the Sabbath day, to keep it holy.

The first thing we need to settle on with this commandment is which day is the Sabbath day. The seventh day of the week is the Sabbath, and using our calendar, that would make it Saturday. Creation was finished in six days, and the Lord rested on the seventh day (Genesis 2:2–3). This day of rest He called the Sabbath day. The word "Sabbath" means a rest and cease from all labors.

Why did the Lord command a day of rest, a Sabbath day? This was to be a holy day to honor a Holy God in a holy manner; it was the LORD'S day. LORD's day, a day of rest when the people of God were to remember their God and what He had done for them. In Exodus 31:13–17, we read that **the Sabbath was a sign between the Israelites and God;** it was to set them apart from other nations and sanctify them to serve the true God, the Creator of all. The Sabbath was created by the LORD as a sign. It was one of the marks of the covenant.

Christians do not keep Saturday as their holy day, a rest day. Jesus was resurrected on the day following the Jewish Sabbath, the first day of the week, Sunday (Matthew 28:1, John 20:1). Therefore, Christians celebrate Sunday as their day of rest (Acts 20:7, 1 Corinthians 16:1–2). We often refer to Sunday as the Lord's Day, and as Christians, we should be ever-mindful of the Lord's Day and not allow it to become like the other days of the week, filled with work and worries. We should set it aside to be a holy day, a day of rest.

Verses from the New Testament:

1 Corinthians 16:2

2 Upon the first day of the week let every one of you lay by him in store, as God hath prospered him, that there be no gatherings when I come. (See also Acts 20:7, Revelation 1:10, Hebrews 10:25.)

Fifth Commandment: Honour thy father and thy mother: that thy days may be long upon the land which the LORD thy God giveth thee.

What does the word "honor" mean? Most of the time, we think of it as obeying our parents, and although this is part of its meaning, it is not the entire meaning. Obeying is the first step in honoring our parents. As children grow, so do the importance and impact of honoring their parents. They should be learning more ways to honor their parents than obedience. Teenagers should be taught to honor by acting respectfully toward their parents in private and in public. How often have we heard young people talk badly about "my old lady" or "the old man" or call their parents by their first names? Disrespect comes in words and actions (rolling eyes and other body language), but neither should be coming from a child who wants to be right with the Lord. As adults, we are still our parents' children and need to honor them by still doing those things that we have been taught, respecting them, and caring for them when they are old and need our help both financially and physically.

This is the only commandment with a promise added to it: that thy days may be long upon the land which the LORD thy God giveth thee. A child who keeps this commandment will have learned to come under the authority and direction of God and will have the blessings of the Lord in his or her life. This commandment is not only for small children but also for anyone because we are all children, regardless of age. Yes, children are commanded to honor their parents; however, there is also a responsibility for the parents to instruct their children in the Lord properly and to be the type of parents who are honorable and can be respected into old age by their children.

Many times, as parents, we want to remind our kids of this commandment, but it would also do well to remind ourselves of Ephesians 6:4: "And, ye fathers, provoke not your children to wrath: but bring them up in the nurture and admonition of the Lord."

Verses from the New Testament:

Colossians 3:20

20 Children, obey your parents in all things: for this is well pleasing unto the Lord. (See also Ephesians 6:1–2; Matthew 15:4, 19:19; Mark 7:10, 10:19; Luke 18:20.)

Sixth Commandment: Thou shalt not kill.

It is interesting to note the placement of this commandment. The first four commandments have to do with our relationship with God. The fifth has to do with our relationship with our earthly parents. The sixth commandment deals with the sanctity of life.

Which brings us to the next point: the definition of the word "kill." "Kill" means murder—premeditated, planned, and willful murder! The best way to understand this verse is to understand what it does not mean. It does not mean a person cannot defend himself from violence (Exodus 22:2), and it does not condemn the death penalty for crimes worthy of death (Exodus 22:18–20). To kill for a reason that is not lawful is murder. "Don't kill" is not a command to prevent the carrying out of God's justice.

It does not mean the duties of a soldier under command to kill in wartime. Many times, Christian soldiers are troubled by thinking they have broken this commandment. They have no need to be troubled. There are accounts in the Old Testament about when the Israelites were commanded and required by the LORD to go and destroy all of the enemies who were in the city. (See also Genesis 9:6; Deuteronomy 25:17–19; 1 Samuel 15:1–3, 18–19.)

"Thou shalt not kill" means not to willfully and maliciously take a person's life. The Lord Himself took it a bit further in the New Testament:

John 3:15

15 Whosoever hateth his brother is a murderer: and ye know that no murderer hath eternal life abiding in him.

The Lord knew the heart of man, and one who hates has the spirit of a murderer, and if he thinks about it long enough, he will act on his hatred and, like Cain, commit murder.

Verses from the New Testament:

Romans 13:9–10

9 For this, Thou shalt not commit adultery, Thou shalt not kill, Thou shalt not steal, Thou shalt not bear false witness, Thou shalt not covet; and if there be any

other commandment, it is briefly comprehended in this saying, namely, Thou shalt love thy neighbour as thyself.

10 Love worketh no ill to his neighbour: therefore love is the fulfilling of the law. (See also Galatians 5:21; Revelation 21:8.)

Seventh Commandment: Thou shalt not commit adultery.

We tend to think of this commandment as dealing only with sex with someone else other than one's spouse; however, it is also dealing with those things that betray marriage vows and with maintaining purity within the union of the couple. Anything that take affection away from spouses within the marriage is harmful. Betrayal and passions for others can be raised through impure pictures, books, and conversations with others besides the marriage partner through e-mails, texts, phone calls, etc.

We see this in the New Testament, where Jesus identified the root of adultery as being a problem with the heart. Matthew 5:28: "But I say unto you, That whosoever looketh on a woman to lust after her hath committed adultery with her already in his heart."

Verses from the New Testament:
Matthew 19:6
6 Wherefore they are no more twain, but one flesh. What therefore God hath joined together, let not man put asunder. (See also Mark 10:7–9.)

Eighth Commandment: Thou shalt not steal.

This commandment seems to be rather simple. However, there really is more to it than taking something that belongs to another. Stealing can be taking things from others by deceit or fraud, not returning what has been borrowed or found, not paying debts or wages, not paying taxes, and taking advantage of someone who is buying or selling something (either giving less or making one pay more). Theft would also apply to kidnapping people for all manner of evil (human trafficking). It also includes the taking away from another his or her good reputation, character, and name (identity theft.) Furthermore, this commandment even reaches spiritual matters—not following through with those things we have promised the Lord we would do for Him (vows), our tithes, and our service.

Verses from the New Testament:

Ephesians 4:28

28 Let him that stole steal no more: but rather let him labour, working with his hands the thing which is good, that he may have to give to him that needeth. (See also 1 Thessalonians 4:6.)

Ninth Commandment: Thou shall not lie.

False witness is anything said with the intent and purpose of bringing injury to a person. Suppressing the truth when known, by which a person may be defrauded of his possessions or his name and character, comes under this commandment. This commandment is easy to understand and gets right to the point. *Spurgeon Devotional Commentary* explains it best: "All lying is herein condemned."

Verses from the New Testament:

Ephesians 4:25

25 Wherefore putting away lying, speak every man truth with his neighbour: for we are members one of another. (See also Ephesians. 4:29.)

Tenth Commandment: Thou shalt not covet.

It is one thing to like and even admire something another has, but this commandment goes beyond that. This commandment is telling us more than not to take what belongs to another person; it also deals with the intent of the heart and the desire to take it. It is just as sinful to steal as it is to lust after something without

62

ever stealing it. Discontent with what we have and envy for what others have is what this commandment forbids. In this last commandment, we see the sin of the heart that deals with the thought and imaginations of a heart that is not content.

Verses from the New Testament:

Hebrews 13:5

5 Let your conversation be without covetousness; and be content with such things as ye have: for he hath said, I will never leave thee, nor forsake thee. (See also 1 Timothy. 6:6.)

Summary

What better way to show someone that he or she is a sinner in need of a Savior than by using the Ten Commandments—whether it be with children or adults. Ask them whether they have ever told a lie, taken the Lord's name in vain, stole something, etc. Usually, by the time you get to the ninth commandment, they are convinced that they are sinners.

Tools for Teaching the Ten Commandments:

Use hand motions to help adult and child students learn the Ten Commandments. Make up your own or check out YouTube videos. Below is a link to one.

https://youtu.be/uZO4dOcQXo8

Lesson 1 Memorization

1. No other gods before Me!
2. Make no images of Me!
3. Don't take My name in vain!
4. Keep the LORD's Day!
5. Honor your parents!
6. Don't murder!
7. Don't commit adultery!
8. Don't steal!
9. Don't lie!
10. Don't covet!

Question 1: What verse in the New Testament explains the purpose of the Law?

Answer: Galatians 3:24! Please write down the verse from memory.

Question 2: Why does commandment four say the LORD's Day instead of the Sabbath?

Answer: It was never about the day—it was about the LORD.

LESSON 2: THE TRIUNITY OF GOD

. . . *Sir, we would see Jesus.* Yes, you will find Him in the triunity of God, for Jesus is the second person of the Godhead.

The triunity of God (commonly referred to as the Trinity) is the main target for all nonbelievers. Among those who consider themselves to be in the mainstream of historical, fundamental Christianity, it is one of the most important doctrines of their faith. One of the reasons that this truth was and is so strongly opposed is that it remained a mystery until the revelation of the person of Jesus Christ, the Eternal Son of God. The Apostle Paul is speaking here in Colossians 1:25–27: "Whereof I am made a minister, according to the dispensation of God which is given to me for you, to fulfil the word of God;" 26 "Even the mystery which hath been hid from ages and from generations, but now is made manifest to his saints:" 27 "To whom God would make known what is the riches of the glory of this mystery among the Gentiles; which is Christ in you, the hope of glory."

This mystery was also hidden in passages like these, which actually began with the very first verse in the Bible:

Genesis 1:1

1 In the beginning God [Elohim, a plural noun that requires a singular verb] created the heaven and the earth.

Genesis 1:26

26 And God [plural noun] said, <u>Let us</u> [plural pronoun] make man in <u>our</u> [relating to us] image, after <u>our likeness</u> [God made man a triune being like Himself].

1 Thessalonians 5:23

23 And the very God of peace sanctify you wholly; and I pray God your whole <u>spirit</u> and <u>soul</u> and <u>body</u>

[the triune nature of man] be preserved blameless unto the coming of our Lord Jesus Christ.

Notice in this verse the word "name." It is singular, not plural. It does not say in the "names" of the Father, Son, and Holy Spirit. It's just another clue to guide the prudent and perplex the scoffers. Matthew 28:19 says, "Go ye therefore, and teach all nations, baptizing them in the <u>name</u> of the Father, and of the Son, and of the Holy Ghost."

The unwillingness of the Jews to believe that Jesus Christ was the Son of God (meaning that He was of the same nature and being as the Father) was one of the reasons they condemned Him for blasphemy and demanded that He be crucified. Consider what Jesus said in the following passage:

John 10:30–33
30 I and my Father are one [in essence and nature].
31 Then the Jews took up stones again to stone him.

32 Jesus answered them, Many good works have I shewed you from my Father; for which of those works do ye stone me?

33 The Jews answered him, saying, For a good work we stone thee not; but for blasphemy; and because that thou, being a man, makest thyself God [or equal to God].

Now consider what the Jews said:

Matthew 26:62–65

62 And the high priest arose, and said unto him, Answerest thou nothing? What is it which these witness against thee?

63 But Jesus held his peace. And the high priest answered and said unto him, I adjure thee by the living God, that thou tell us whether thou be the Christ, the Son of God.

64 Jesus saith unto him, Thou hast said [Yes, I am!]: nevertheless I say unto you, Hereafter shall ye see the

Son of man sitting on the right hand of power, and coming in the clouds of heaven.

65 Then the high priest rent his clothes, saying, <u>He hath spoken blasphemy; what further need have we of witnesses? Behold, now ye have heard his blasphemy</u>.

Because the deity of Christ and the triunity of God are targets of controversy for nonbelievers, Christians should be able to give an answer to anyone who asks a reason for their beliefs. Here are statements that the Bible supports.

Trinity

A word used to speak of the eternal relationship of the members of the Godhead—God the Father, God the Son, and God the Holy Spirit. The simplest expression of this truth is the answer to this question: how can one explain the Trinity? It is the belief that God is one eternal being in three eternal persons. It can also be expressed in this manner: in the Godhead, there are three Persons. Each Person is fully God. There is only one God. What is the Godhead? The Godhead is a collective term that speaks of God the Father, God the Son, and God the Holy Spirit. Christ is said to be the fullness of the Godhead bodily, as expressed in Colossians 2:9: "For in him [Jesus Christ] dwelleth all the fulness of the Godhead bodily." The Bible supports the previous and following statement doctrinally.

71

The Father is called God (John 6:27). "Labour not for the meat which perisheth, but for that meat which endureth unto everlasting life, which the Son of man shall give unto you: for him hath God the Father sealed."

Jesus is called God (John 1:1). "$_{1a}$ In the beginning was the Word, $_{1b}$ and the Word was with God, $_{1c}$ and the Word [title for Jesus] was God [a god is a false rendering of John $_{1c}$ and a contradiction to John 20:28 and many other verses]."

The Holy Spirit is called God (Acts 5:3–4). "But Peter said, Ananias, why hath Satan filled thine heart to lie to the Holy Ghost, and to keep back part of the price of the land?" 4 "Hast thou conceived this thing in thine heart? Thou hast not lied unto men, but unto God."

There is only one God (1 Timothy 2:5). "For there is one God, and one mediator between God and men, the man Christ Jesus."

God created man in His image and likeness (Genesis 1:26–27). "And God said, Let us make man in our image, after our likeness: and let them have dominion over the fish of the sea, and over the fowl of the air, and over the cattle, and over all the earth, and over every creeping thing that creepeth upon the earth." 27 "So God created man in his own image, in the image of God created he him; male and female created he them."

There is only one man (1 Thessalonians 5:23). "And the very God of peace sanctify you [the man or person] wholly; and I pray God your whole spirit and soul and body be preserved blameless unto the coming of our Lord Jesus Christ."

1. God is triune. He is one eternal being in three eternal persons.

2. God created man in His own image and likeness.

3. Man is triune. He is wholly man (not animal-like). There is only one man.

Observations

Why do we believe that the Father is God? Because the Bible calls Him God.

Why do we believe that the Son (Jesus Christ) is God? Because the Bible calls Him God.

Why do we believe that the Holy Spirit is God? Because the Bible calls Him God.

Why do we believe that there is only one God? Because the Bible declares that there is only one God.

Conclusion

Whereas the Bible calls the Father God, the Son God, and the Holy Spirit God and states that there is only one God, we must conclude that the Bible teaches that there is one Eternal God who is triune.

When the New Testament was completed, the mystery of the triunity of God was unveiled. God the Father sent His Son to be the sacrifice for all who would receive Him by faith. God the Son (Jesus Christ) became flesh and dwelt among us, and was crucified, buried, and resurrected on the third day after His death. He sent God the Holy Spirit to dwell in each child of God. What a blessing it is to believe these truths, and what an awesome God He is!

Lesson 2 Memorization

Question 1: What does the word "Trinity" mean?

Answer: It is a word used to speak of the eternal relationship of the members of the Godhead—God the Father, God the Son, and God the Holy Spirit.

Question 2: Why do we believe that the Father is God? Give the verse that states that the Father is God.

Answer: We believe that the Father is God because the Bible calls Him God (John 6:27).

Question 3: Why do we believe that Jesus is God? Give five verses that state that Jesus is God.

Answer: We believe that Jesus is God because the Bible calls Him God (Isaiah 9:6, John 1:1, John 20:28, 1 Timothy 3:16, Revelation 1:7–8).

Question 4: Why do we believe that the Holy Spirit is God? Give four verses that show this truth.

Answer: We believe that the Holy Spirit is God because the Bible calls Him God (Acts 5:3–4, 1 John 4:15, John 14:16–17, Romans 8:9).

Question 5: Could you explain the Trinity?

Answer: It is the belief that God is one eternal being in three eternal Persons. It can also be expressed in this manner: in the Godhead, there are three Persons. Each Person is fully God. There is only one God.

Question 6: What is the Godhead?

Answer: The Godhead is a word that speaks of God the Father, God the Son, and God the Holy Spirit. Christ is said to be the fullness of the Godhead bodily.

As Colossians 2:9 says, "For in him [Jesus Christ] dwelleth all the fulness of the Godhead bodily."

Question 7: What is the greatest evidence in creation that God is a triune being?

Answer: God's creation of man is the greatest evidence in creation that He is triune, for He created man in His own image and likeness. As Genesis 1:26–27 says: 26 "And God said, Let us make man in our image, after our likeness: and let them have dominion over the fish of the sea, and over the fowl of the air, and over the cattle, and over all the earth, and over every creeping thing that creepeth upon the earth." 27 "So God created man in his own image, in the image of God created he him; male and female created he them."

LESSON 3: THE ARMOR OF GOD

. . . Sir, we would see Jesus. Yes, you will find Him in combat, for the battle is the Lord's.

Christians bear your armor—Ephesians 6:10–17! The command to put on the whole armor of God is seldom taken seriously. Very few people from pew to pew, in most churches, could even name the pieces of armor because they are yet to have the skills to enter battle with them. Bearing armor takes much more effort than just memorizing the list of armor. It takes combat training from someone who is a veteran soldier. That someone must take on the role of a leader who's been on the front lines long enough to know both victory and defeat. The first step in taking this lesson into application is knowing the pieces of armor and then becoming skillful with each of them. This is where your permanent memory will serve you well.

The seven (six visible, one invisible) different pieces of spiritual armor are compared to the actual pieces of armor for a Roman soldier:

1. Loins girt with truth—the soldier's belt keeps things in place

2. Breastplate of righteousness—protects the soldier's heart

3. Feet shod with the gospel of peace—genius of spiked sandals

4. Shield of faith—to protect from the seen and unseen enemy

5. Helmet of salvation—bronze, lined with leather, neck cover

6. Sword of the Spirit—two-edged, turned up at the tip

7. Prayer in the Spirit—a Christian soldier's mental and physical strength

Truth = knowing God's will and the 10 basic doctrines of the faith to keep all the other parts of the armor in place.

Righteousness = being right with the Lord and your fellow man to make the heart function at full capacity.

Gospel = God's incredible plan of redemption and way of peace.

Faith = the victory shield that protects us from all our enemies.

Salvation = everlasting life that no enemy can take from us.

God's Word = the power that transforms a life.

Prayer = the most powerful, invisible weapon that the enemy cannot see, which brings victory in battle. No war has ever been won by weapons or strategy alone. It takes the whole armor of God to win.

For all Christians to stand in the battles encountered during their lives, they must put on the whole armor of God. All seven weapons must be in place and functioning! Our Captain is Jesus.

Lesson 3 Memorization

Write or say the seven pieces of armor from memory and explain how they will enable you to stand against your enemies.

LESSON 4: THE BASIC DOCTRINES

. . . Sir, we would see Jesus. Yes, you will find Him in doctrine, for Jesus said that if anyone would do the Father's will, he would know that His doctrine was of God.

Undoubtedly, this lesson will be the most demanding and time-consuming, but it is also one of the most essential and rewarding when finished. Learning the 10 basic doctrines of the Christian faith immediately puts you in the class of the elite. Memorizing them will plant them in your mind. Knowing how to apply them hermeneutically will place you among the rarest of jewels. Your price will be higher than rubies. You will have a foundation that's built upon rock, rock that will stand the tests of besieging rain, floods, and blowing winds. This pillar of faith, that you will have built upon God's Word, will enable the sweet Lord Jesus to use you in ways beyond your wildest dreams. Yes, all that and so much more. What makes this incredible task possible for people of all ages is desire. God knows your heart. If it's truly your desire to learn this lesson for His honor and glory, it's yours regardless of whether you're young or older. Just take a look at what your Lord has promised you in Psalms 37:4–5: "Delight thyself also in the LORD; and he shall give thee the <u>desires of thine heart</u>." 5 "Commit thy way unto the LORD; trust also in him; and he shall bring it to pass."

That's a promise you can count on anytime. So are you ready to get started?

It may take a class six months to a year to reach the permanent memory with this lesson. Once one or two people have the five points of the first doctrine down, then they will begin working to help other classmates. I started like this:

Creator

Triune

Eternal

Spirit

Love

I would write this list as many times as necessary to make it automatically recallable in both my writing and speaking. Next, write the Scriptures next to each item in the list. Keep doing this until you've got it. Do it every day. Think about it while you're driving to work. In any spare moment you have, think about it. Say it to yourself. Write it down or say it out loud. Once you have the first doctrine down, always say it first as you begin learning the second, third, and so on. That's it! There's nothing more to it than that—other than saying, "O Lord, I need You to enable me to do this; I can't do it without You, Lord, and when it's all done, I will give You all the praise, honor, and glory."

(1) THEOLOGY—THE STUDY OF GOD

1. God Is Creator - Gen 1:1
2. God Is Triune - Gen 1:26

3. God Is Eternal - Ps 90:2

4. God Is Spirit - John 4:24

5. God Is Love - 1 John 4:16

(2) CHRISTOLOGY—THE STUDY OF CHRIST

1. Christ Is Creator - John 1:3, Col 1:16

2. Christ Is Jehovah God - Zech 12:10

3. Christ Is Eternal - John 1:1, Heb 7:3

4. Christ Is Our Sinbearer - 1 John 2:2

5. Christ Is Unchanging - Heb 13:8

(3) PNEUMATOLOGY—THE STUDY OF THE HOLY SPIRIT

1. He Is Creator - Gen 1:2

2. He Is God - Acts 5:4, 1 John 4:15, John 14:15–16, Rom 8:9

3. He Is Eternal - Heb 9:14

4. He Is a Person - John 16:7–8

5. He Is the Regenerator - Titus 3:5

(4) ANGELOLOGY—THE STUDY OF ANGELS

1. Created - Ps 148:5
2. Fallen - Isa 14:12, Ezk 28:11–19
3. Sentenced - Matt 25:41, Rev 20:10
4. Holy - Matt 25:31
5. Spirits - Heb 1:13–14

(5) ANTHROPOLOGY—THE STUDY OF MAN

1. Created - Gen 2:7
2. Immortal - Eccl 12:7
3. Inexcusable - Rom 1:20
4. Lost - Gen 2:17, Rom 5:12
5. Saved - Acts 16:31

(6) BIBLIOLOGY—THE STUDY OF SCRIPTURE

1. Its Plenary Verbal Inspiration - Jer 1:9, 2 Tim 3:16
2. Its Author - 2 Peter 1:20–21
3. Its Power - Heb 4:12, Rom 10:17

4. Its Preservation - John 12:48, Rev 20:12

5. Its Place - Ps 138:2

(7) HAMARTIOLOGY—THE STUDY OF SIN

1. Origin - Isa 14:12–17, Ezk 28:17

2. Fact - Gen 6:5, John 16:8

3. Nature - Rom 6:23

4. Consequence - Matt 13:15

5. Universality - Isa 53:6

(8) SOTERIOLOGY—THE STUDY OF SALVATION

1. Not in Religion - Mark 7:7–9

2. Not in Works - Rom 4:4–5

3. Not in Morality - Isa 64:6

4. But in a Person - John 14:6

5. And in a Relationship - John 3:5

(9) ECCLESIOLOGY—THE STUDY OF THE CHURCH

1. Its Beginning - Acts 2:41

2. Its Head - Eph 5:23

3. Its Purpose - Acts 1:8

4. Its Leadership - 1 Tim 3:1–16, Titus 2:1–12

5. Its Removal - 1 Thess 4:13–14

(10) ESCHATOLOGY—THE STUDY OF LAST THINGS

1. The Great Tribulation - Rev 6–18

2. The Second Coming of Christ - Rev 19

3. The Millennium - Rev 20

4. The Last Judgment - Rev 20:11–15

5. The Eternal State - Rev 21–22

Lesson 4 Memorization

Write or say each of the 10 doctrines by name and give the five subpoints with their Scripture references. This may be your greatest challenge, but you can be assured that it will also be your greatest reward. Once your loins are girded with truth, the Lord will use you in ways that you may have never imagined. May the sweet Lord Jesus bless you richly as you delight in His Word.

SECTION 2: LESSONS FOR GROWTH

Lesson 5: Walking with God

Lesson 6: Adding to Your Faith

Lesson 7: Think on These Things

Lesson 8: The Love Doctrine

LESSON 5: WALKING WITH GOD

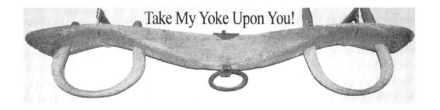

Take My Yoke Upon You!

. . . *Sir, we would see Jesus.* Yes, you will find Him in the way, for Jesus has invited you to take His yoke upon you and walk with Him each day.

Do you know anything about the people mentioned in the Bible who walked with God? First of all, they were people just like you and me. There is only one thing that makes any saved person different from those who walked with God. That one thing is just a little word, but it means a lot to Him. That word is **desire**. People who walk with God do so because they have the **desire** to be close to Him. Consider the implications of this verse, James 4:8: "Draw nigh to God, and he will draw nigh to you." It's that simple! But to do that, you must have a pure heart. A pure heart is a heart that is free from all unconfessed sin and anything else that would hinder your fellowshipping with a Thrice-Holy God who is your Heavenly Father. **Desire** is the key to making this possible. Take His yoke upon you and walk with Him every day. Delight in His presence.

Here are two references in Scripture that talk about people who enjoyed walking with the Lord Jesus Christ before His Incarnation. By the way, LORD written in all caps in the Old Testament is the personal name for God, which is commonly known today as Yahweh. In most references, it is Jesus Christ appearing as a Christophany (Jesus in a bodily form before His Incarnation). He is also referred to many times as the Angel of the LORD.

Genesis 5:21–24

21 And Enoch lived sixty and five years, and begat Methuselah:

22 And <u>Enoch walked with God</u> after he begat Methuselah three hundred years, and begat sons and daughters:

23 And all the days of Enoch were three hundred sixty and five years:

24 And <u>Enoch walked with God</u>: and he was not; for God took him.

How long was it before Enoch walked with God? It was 65 years. There's a lot missing in this story that would be very interesting to know. How did Enoch get saved? How long after Enoch knew the LORD was it that he learned to walk with Him? There are many more questions that one could think of that will have to wait until we see him in glory. And that part about God taking Enoch—that's my favorite.

Well, the next story about Noah has quite a different ending, yet to me, it is far more dramatic. If you're an animal lover, you might enjoy the voyage. On the other hand, if you are prone to sea sickness, the thought could induce nightmares. Walking with God has the components not only of desire and purity but also of faith. Desire, combined with faith and a pure heart, is what makes one's walk with the Lord a reality. Think of the great privilege that Noah had to walk with his Creator, who would recreate a new world right before his very eyes.

Genesis 6:7–9

7 And the LORD said, I will destroy man whom I have created from the face of the earth; both man, and beast, and the creeping things, and the fowls of the air; for it repenteth me that I have made them.

8 But Noah found grace in the eyes of the LORD.

9 These are the generations of Noah: Noah was a just man and perfect in his generations, and <u>Noah walked with God</u>.

Now, as we move to the New Testament, the walk with God is so much more profound, so much more personal, and so much more passionate. Could you imagine yourself as Mary, His mother; Joseph, His step-father; or one of His followers? "Walking with God" took on a whole new dimension during the years that He walked this earth. Can you imagine yourself in the very presence of the LORD God of heaven and earth?

Until we have the overwhelming joy of walking with Him in His Kingdom of righteousness described in Revelation 21, we children of God are invited to walk with Him now by yoking up each day. The yoke is used as a metaphor to describe how the Lord can ease the burden of the one walking with Him. He said that His yoke is easy and that His burden is light.

Matthew 11:28–30

28 Come unto me, all ye that labour and are heavy laden, and I will give you rest.

29 Take my yoke upon you, and learn of me; for I am meek and lowly in heart: and ye shall find rest unto your souls.

30 For my yoke is easy, and my burden is light.

This passage is not only an invitation for sinners who are lost but also an invitation for all those who are bearing their burdens during the heat of the day. It is a day when Jesus said the world would be like the days of Noah and like the days of Sodom and Gomorrah. And it is a day when good would be called evil and evil would be called good. I don't know about you, but I need His help. Christians have to wear a hard yoke that this wicked world has placed upon them and a heavy burden of care that make their journeys tiresome. We need Him to help us lighten our burdens. If you yoke up with the Lord each day, you will never walk alone. His presence will not only be in you, but it will also be with you in everything that you do. Enjoy the walk, pilgrim!

Lesson 5 Memorization

Question 1: What are the three requirements that make it possible to walk with God?

Answer: The three requirements are to know Him by the means of a spiritual birth into the family of God, to have the desire to walk with Him, and to obey His Word.

Question 2: Which of the three requirements will prove most likely to enable you to succeed?

Answer: Desire!

Enjoy your walk with the sweet Lord Jesus every day.

LESSON 6: ADDING TO YOUR FAITH

. . . Sir, we would see Jesus. Yes, you will find Him in the steps of spiritual growth, for Jesus is personified in each of the seven steps.

2 Peter 1:5–8

5 And beside this, giving all diligence, add to your faith virtue; and to virtue knowledge;

6 And to knowledge temperance; and to temperance patience; and to patience godliness;

7 And to godliness brotherly kindness; and to brotherly kindness charity.

8 For if these things be in you, and abound, they make you that ye shall neither be barren nor unfruitful in the knowledge of our Lord Jesus Christ.

Maturity does not happen overnight. It takes time to develop into a mature Christian. In 2 Peter 1:5–8, we see the progression of maturity in the life of a Christian. Those steps are faith; virtue; knowledge;

temperance; patience; Godliness; brotherly kindness; and finally, charity. Christian growth takes place as you progress through these seven steps.

Faith (saving faith) is an act of the heart and is generated by trust. God has proven Himself trustworthy; therefore, we should trust Him.

Virtue is a strong desire to do right; it is Biblical morality. The desire to want to do right will lead one to the next step.
(1 Corinthians 5:15, Proverbs 4:23)

Knowledge is what one knows. Studying the Bible, memorizing Scripture, and learning the fundamentals of the faith are vital to Christian growth. Knowledge of spiritual truths is gained through the study of Scripture.
(2 Timothy 2:2, 2 Timothy 2:15, Psalms 119:89, 1 John 4:1)

Temperance is self-control. It is taking what we learn through knowledge and putting those truths into action. This requires work on the part of the Christian and reliance on the Holy Spirit to be our guide instead of our old nature before we were saved. (John 16:13)

Patience is persevering in trials cheerfully and without complaint. Patience is received and learned through enduring tribulations (Romans 5:3–5) and through the trying of our faith (James 1:3–4). It is through these that we learn patience, for we learn to trust the Lord completely and accept His will for us because we trust in His goodness, wisdom, and faithfulness.

Godliness is Christ-likeness in our lives: complete devotion to, reliance on, and confidence in the Lord resulting in contentment (1 Timothy 6:6). We see examples of this in the lives of Job and Paul (Job 1:21–22; Philippians 1:21, 4:11–13). These men learned godliness. They depended completely on the

Lord. They endured hardships because of the oneness they had with the Lord.

Brotherly kindness is kindness or love shown to one's brethren. Up to this point in spiritual growth, the growth has been between the Christian and the Lord, but now it is extended to others in the body of Christ—regardless of race, culture, or background. This has to do with unity within the body of Christ (Psalms 133:10). We read in John 13:34–35 that the world will know we are Christians by our love for our brethren. Christ is our example of brotherly kindness (Ephesians 4:32).

Charity is love, but it is agape love. This love is an active love and extends from the heart to all mankind. The Lord would have us continue expressing His agape love to a lost world so that all men come to salvation. Charity is a sincere desire to see people saved and to see them become discipled and mature spiritually (Matthew 28:19–20).

Spiritual maturity is possible, one step at a time:

FAITH = saving faith, then adding to your faith

VIRTUE = Biblical morality, putting off

KNOWLEDGE = of spiritual truths

TEMPERANCE = self-control, truths in action

PATIENCE = perseverance in trials

GODLINESS = Christ-likeness

BROTHERLY KINDNESS = extended hands

CHARITY = agape love, extended heart

ARE THESE THINGS ABOUNDING IN YOU?

Christian growth takes place as you progress through these seven steps. The next step may not be possible until you have mastered the previous one.

WHERE ARE YOU RIGHT NOW?

Lesson 6 Memorization

Please list or recite from memory the seven things we Christians are to add to our faith and give the definition of each.

VIRTUE = Biblical morality, putting off

KNOWLEDGE = of spiritual truths

TEMPERANCE = self-control, truths in action

PATIENCE = perseverance in trials

GODLINESS = Christ-likeness

BROTHERLY KINDNESS = extended hands

CHARITY = agape love, extended heart

LESSON 7: THINK ON THESE THINGS

. . . Sir, we would see Jesus. Yes, you will find Him in the words to think on, for Jesus is the perfect picture of them all.

Philippians 4:8

8 Finally, brethren, whatsoever things are <u>true</u>, whatsoever things are <u>honest</u>, whatsoever things are <u>just</u>, whatsoever things are <u>pure</u>, whatsoever things are <u>lovely</u>, whatsoever things are of <u>good report</u>; if there be any <u>virtue</u>, and if there be any <u>praise</u>, **think on these things**.

The first thing we need to understand is "think" in this verse. It means more than just an occasional thought about something. It means to take an inventory, esteem, reason, reckon.

The things we think on are the very things that turn into actions in our everyday lives. Jesus said:

Mark 7:20–24

20 And he said, That which cometh out of the man, that defileth the man.

21 For from within, out of the heart of men, proceed evil thoughts, adulteries, fornications, murders,

22 Thefts, covetousness, wickedness, deceit, lasciviousness, an evil eye, blasphemy, pride, foolishness:

23 All these evil things come from within, and defile the man.

In this passage, we learn what we should think on and put into practice to live lives that are pleasing to the Lord. The first thing Paul tells us to think on is truth. What is truth for Christians? Truth comes from the Lord. The opposite of truth is falseness, and it does not come from Him. Jesus tells us that He is truth in John 14:6: "Jesus saith unto him, I am the way, the truth, and the life: no man cometh unto the Father, but by me."

Thinking on truth will bring perfect peace to us, as mentioned in Isaiah 26:3: "Thou will keep him in perfect peace, whose mind is stayed on thee: because he trusteth in thee."

The next thing we are told to think on is those things that are honest. "Honest," in this verse, means that which is reverent or honorable. The word "honest" has to do with Christians personally and doing those things that would earn respect in regard to business dealings as well as having the proper respect and honor for the customs of society and culture when they do not violate Christians' conscience or the laws of God.

(Romans 12:2, 17; 2 Corinthians 8:21; 1 Timothy 3:7; 1 Thessalonians 5:15; 1 Peter 3:9; Galatians 6:8; Romans 12:17)

Think on those things that are just. Being just is doing those things that are right between you and others. Christians should be just in all their dealings with others. The world measures a man's Christian character and integrity by his practices of justice and honesty more than by his ability to quote Scripture or how frequently he attends church.

Think on those things that are pure. The word "pure" means that which is innocent, modest, and clean; it is also in reference to the state of mind and the acts of the body. We often think of purity as having to do with those things we allow into our lives as actions; however, our state of mind is also involved in the word "pure."

Unchaste behavior can and often does destroy one's life; thinking about impure things will also destroy one. As Christians, we need to think on those things that are pure and not entertain thoughts of things that are not.

Think on those things that are lovely. Using the word "lovely" is interesting because it means to think on those things that are friendly toward others—acceptable, amiable, and agreeable to others. One should not have a sour attitude or a crabby temper, especially toward others. We should not find fault in everything and everyone who has no piety. A person who has a kind disposition in his words and actions will have the greatest effect and be a lasting influence on others. We need to think on how we come across to others and work on being lovely.

Think on things that are of good report. The phrase "good report" means well spoken of or reputable. Those things that we do should be well spoken of by both the lost and Christians. A good report should be a reputation that is known to be mannerly, respectful, courteous, and kind.

We should maintain a good report from those around us, not for vainglory or the applause of men but rather for the honor and glory of our Lord and Savior, Jesus Christ, and to further the gospel message.

This passage ends with this admonition: "If there be any virtue, and if there be any praise, think on these things." No doubt, Paul knows he has not given a full list of virtues that need to be cultivated in Christians' lives, so now he adds that, if there be any virtue, anything else that will develop Christian excellence and praise, we must think (diligently consider and practice—make them a part of our lives) on these things.

Summary

As we commit Philippians 4:8 to memory, we also need to meditate on these positive thoughts daily. Jonathan Edwards said, "The ideas and images in men's minds are the invisible powers that constantly govern them."

With the help of the Holy Spirit through His Word, we Christians are able to keep our minds free from sinful thoughts. By committing those things learned to permanent memory we are able to have a life that is pleasing to men and the Lord.

We have all heard the story of the old Indian explaining to his young son the battle inside all of us. "There is a black dog fighting with a white dog inside of me every day." The young son asked him which one wins, and his father wisely answered, "The one I feed the most."

Lesson 7 Memorization

Please list or say the eight things that will keep your mind filled with positive thoughts. The prime examples are:

1. True
2. Honest
3. Just
4. Pure
5. Lovely
6. Good Report
7. If There Be Any Virtue
8. If There Be Any Praise

. . . Think on these things.

LESSON 8: THE LOVE DOCTRINE

. . . *Sir, we would see Jesus.* Yes, you will find Him in the love doctrine, for Jesus is the love of God Incarnate.

The love of God is without measure. Understanding its vastness is like standing on a bridge that spans all the oceans of the world and trying to explore its contents one bucket at a time. The permanent-memory portion of it will be taken from 1 Corinthians 13, but before we get there, we can draw a few buckets from these other three passages of Scripture.

The first one has been given the title the Royal Commandment:

Matthew 22:35–39
35 Then one of them, which was a lawyer, asked him a question, tempting him, and saying,

36 Master, which is the <u>great commandment</u> in the law?

37 Jesus said unto him, Thou shalt love the Lord thy God with all thy heart, and with all thy soul, and with all thy mind.

38 This is the first and great commandment.

39 And the second is like unto it, Thou shalt love thy neighbour as thyself.

40 On these two commandments hang all the law and the prophets.

So the first and greatest commandment is to love God with all your heart, soul, and mind. This expresses the idea of loving Him with all your being. The second is to love others in the same way that you love (care for) yourself. The applications here are endless, and the only thing that limits one's practice of this is self-centeredness.

The next passage is given again by the Lord Jesus Himself:

Matthew 5:43–48

43 Ye have heard that it hath been said, Thou shalt love thy neighbour, and hate thine enemy.

44 But I say unto you, <u>Love your enemies, bless them that curse you, do good to them that hate you, and pray for them which despitefully use you, and persecute you;</u>

45 That ye may be the children of your Father which is in heaven: for he maketh his sun to rise on the evil and on the good, and sendeth rain on the just and on the unjust.

46 For if ye love them which love you, what reward have ye? do not even the publicans the same?

47 And if ye salute your brethren only, what do ye more than others? do not even the publicans so?

48 Be ye therefore perfect, even as your Father which is in heaven is perfect.

Are you beginning to feel the gravity of the subject? When the Lord spoke to His disciples about forgiving those who would have sinned against them seven times in a day, they said, "Lord, increase our faith." So it is with us likewise. Lord, increase our faith!

The third passage is actually a text for anyone who claims to be saved. The idea here is that, if one is saved, God dwells in one's heart and that the love of God is there too, which is a testament to a genuine conversion. With God's indwelling presence, a truly born-again child of God will have a love not only for God but also for his or her brothers and sisters in Christ.

1 John 4:7–21

7 Beloved, let us love one another: for love is of God; and every one that loveth is born of God, and knoweth God.

8 He that loveth not knoweth not God; for God is love.

9 In this was manifested the love of God toward us, because that God sent his only begotten Son into the world, that we might live through him.

10 Herein is love, not that we loved God, but that he loved us, and sent his Son to be the propitiation for our sins.

11 Beloved, if God so loved us, we ought also to love one another.

12 No man hath seen God at any time. If we love one another, God dwelleth in us, and his love is perfected in us.

13 Hereby know we that we dwell in him, and he in us, because he hath given us of his Spirit.

14 And we have seen and do testify that the Father sent the Son to be the Saviour of the world.

15 Whosoever shall confess that Jesus is the Son of God, God dwelleth in him, and he in God.

16 And we have known and believed the love that God hath to us. God is love; and he that dwelleth in love dwelleth in God, and God in him.

17 Herein is our love made perfect, that we may have boldness in the day of judgment: because as he is, so are we in this world.

18 There is no fear in love; but perfect love casteth out fear: because fear hath torment. He that feareth is not made perfect in love.

19 We love him, because he first loved us.

20 If a man say, I love God, and hateth his brother, he is a liar: for he that loveth not his brother whom he hath seen, how can he love God whom he hath not seen?

21 And this commandment have we from him, That he who loveth God love his brother also.

After reading these verses, you should be able to honestly judge yourself and know whether you are saved or lost.

From all that the Lord has given us in the love doctrine, we learn to have a greater and more appreciative understanding of how limitless God's love really is.

Now we reach the text that will frame the seven warnings and 16 points that express what charity is. The memorization part of the love doctrine comes from these verses. May the sweet Lord bless you richly as you commit them to your heart.

1 Corinthians 13:1–8

1 Though I speak with the tongues of men and of angels, and have not charity, I am become as sounding brass, or a tinkling cymbal.

2 And though I have the gift of prophecy, and understand all mysteries, and all knowledge; and though I have all faith, so that I could remove mountains, and have not charity, I am nothing.

3 And though I bestow all my goods to feed the poor, and though I give my body to be burned, and have not charity, it profiteth me nothing.

4 Charity suffereth long, and is kind; charity envieth not; charity vaunteth not itself, is not puffed up,

5 Doth not behave itself unseemly, seeketh not her own, is not easily provoked, thinketh no evil;

6 Rejoiceth not in iniquity, but rejoiceth in the truth; [in the truth, or with the truth]

7 Beareth all things, believeth all things, hopeth all things, endureth all things.

8 Charity never faileth: but whether there be prophecies, they shall fail; whether there be tongues, they shall cease; whether there be knowledge, it shall vanish away.

In chapter 12 of 1 Corinthians, the Apostle Paul is instructing the Corinthian Christians about the diversities of spiritual gifts. In chapter 13, he reminds them that the greatest of all those gifts is love. He ends the chapter with a bit of a rebuke and admonition as he tells them that they do not need to contend with one another over who has or what is the best gift, for he is going to show them a more excellent way, and that is charity (love). This is where chapter 13 begins. Paul begins this chapter by stating the seven warnings of not having charity:

1. Speak with tongues of men and angels and have not charity, I am as sounding brass, or tinkling cymbal.
2. Gift of prophecy and have not charity, I am nothing.
3. Gift of understanding all mysteries and have not charity, I am nothing.

4. Gift of all knowledge and have not charity, I am nothing.
5. Gift of all faith and have not charity, I am nothing.
6. Give all my goods to feed the poor and have not charity, I am nothing.
7. Give my body to be burned and have not charity, it profits me nothing.

Then, Paul continues to tell them what charity is and does:

1. Charity suffers long (is long with patience).
2. Charity is kind (acts benevolently).

3. Charity envies not (is not jealous).

4. Charity vaunts not itself (does not brag about itself or its accomplishments).

5. Charity is not puffed up (is not arrogant).

6. Charity does not behave itself unseemly (is not rude).

7. Charity seeks not her own (is not self-centered).

8. Charity is not easily provoked (is not touchy or quick-tempered).

9. Charity thinks no evil (does not keep record of wrongs or evil).

10. Charity rejoices not in iniquity (not in injustice and unrighteousness).

11. Charity does rejoice in truth.

12. Charity bears all things (puts up with injuries without becoming angry).

13. Charity believes all things (believes well of others and does not entertain gossip).

14. Charity hopes in all things (hopes well in all things).

15. Charity endures in all things (suffers well and perseveres under persecutions).

16. Charity never fails (will never become ineffective).

Summary

In 1 Corinthians 14, Paul begins the chapter by telling the Corinthians to follow charity. Make charity a lifelong pursuit and seek to acquire it. As you memorize these 16 points and begin to put them into practice, your life will change. Those who reach this step of Christian maturity will have the greatest joy and reward at the judgment seat of Christ.

Lesson 8 Memorization

Write or say the 16 points of the love doctrine and the seven warnings.

SECTION 3: LESSONS FOR WORKERS

Lesson 9: Ministry for Men and Women

Lesson 10: Hermeneutics 101

Lesson 11: Figures of Speech

Lesson 12: Homiletics 101

LESSON 9: MINISTRY FOR MEN AND WOMEN

. . . Sir, we would see Jesus. Yes, you will find Him in ministry, for Jesus came not to be ministered to, but to minister to others.

This lesson is divided into two sections: WOMEN IN LEADERSHIP and MEN IN MINISTRY. It is intended especially for those who may be in the first steps of preparing to be pastors, evangelists, or missionaries. In most cases, that would include their spouses as well—women in ministry. Because it is both customary and chivalrous for ladies to go first, "Putter" will begin with some of the experiences and lessons that have shaped her life. I am sure the ladies will find them most beneficial. So here it comes, straight from "Putter's" pen.

Women in Leadership

There are in 1 Timothy 3:1–10 definite qualifications for a man who desires to be in a leadership role within the church. Qualifications for the role of women in leadership are not so plainly laid out in Scripture. We can, however, search the Word and find many qualities that a woman in leadership should possess. In Genesis, we find the first mention of a quality that she should possess and what she will need to be effective in any ministry within the church.

Submission

We read in Genesis 3:16: "Unto the woman he said, I will greatly multiply thy sorrow and thy conception; in sorrow thou shalt bring forth children; and thy desire shall be to thy husband, and he shall rule over thee."

From the beginning of time as we know it, the Lord has always established an order within His creation. The New Testament makes mention of this order in 1 Corinthians 11:3: "But I would have you know, that the head of every man is Christ; and the head of the woman is the man; and the head of Christ is God."

Submission to God's order is taught in Ephesians 5:20–24: 20 "Giving thanks always for all things unto God and the Father in the name of our Lord Jesus Christ;" 21 "Submitting yourselves one to another in the fear of God." 22 "Wives, submit yourselves unto your own husbands, as unto the Lord." 23 For the husband is the head of the wife, even as Christ is the head of the church: and he is the saviour of the body." 24 "Therefore as the church is subject unto Christ, so let the wives be to their own husbands in every thing."

Submission is a God-ordained order, and any woman who wants to serve the Lord needs to have an attitude and a heart that submits to the men the Lord has placed over her. This would be her father, husband, pastor, and other men in leadership roles within the church body. As long as these men follow God and His divine ways, principles, and precepts, she is to come under submission to them; however, in no way does this mean that she does not have an opinion or is a doormat, a slave, or beneath a man in any way, for she was created to be a "help meet" (suitable helper) for man, and we are all one in Christ Jesus. Enough said . . . moving right along.

Galatians 3:26–28

26 For ye are all the children of God by faith in Christ Jesus.

27 For as many of you as have been baptized into Christ have put on Christ.

28 There is neither Jew nor Greek, there is neither bond nor free, there is neither male nor female: for ye are all one in Christ Jesus.

Often, a woman will find herself under the authority of another woman in a ministry. She will still need to have a submissive spirit. To be submissive merely means to yield your own will to those who have authority over you. Another very good definition of submission is "a voluntary attitude of cooperation" (Pastor Shane Roberson).

It is easy to understand why submission is the first quality that should characterize the life and actions of a woman who wants to serve the Lord and be in a position of leadership. Otherwise, she would have the opposite qualities: rebellious, contentious, hard-headed, proud, disobedient, and stubborn.

Another well-known passage of Scripture that describes what a woman in leadership should be like is found in Proverbs 31. Yes, we all know about Victorious Vicky, as I like to call her. Even though Vicky has been the envied enemy of women since Solomon penned these words, she really does give us a good insight into what a woman who wants to serve the Lord should have: priorities.

The first thing we read about her is that her price is far above rubies (she is priceless) because, as we read in verse 11, "The heart of her husband doth safely trust in her, so that he shall have no need of spoil," which is interesting considering Genesis 3:16. Because of her priorities being in order, her husband and children rise up and call her blessed—not her pastor, church leaders, or community, but rather her husband and children. Verse 28 says, "Her children arise up, and call her blessed; her husband also, and he praiseth her." Any woman desiring to have a leadership role must make sure her family and home are not neglected; they must be the first on her priority list.

It goes without saying that, spiritually, the Lord has preeminence in our lives, so we must follow the Lord's will for ministry and position within the body of Christ. Too often, these things get out of order, especially when the demands of the ministry and the needs of others are so great.

We see this in the following verses:

1 Corinthians 11:3

3 But I would have you know, that the head of every man is Christ; and the head of the woman is the man; and the head of Christ is God.

Ephesians 5:23

23 For the husband is the head of the wife, even as Christ is the head of the church: and he is the saviour of the body.

Colossians 1:18

18 And he is the head of the body, the church: who is the beginning, the firstborn from the dead; that in all things he might have the preeminence.

Character

When we come to the New Testament, there are many other verses we read that give more insight into what is required of a woman in a position of leadership. These verses can also be summed up in one word: character. One's character is one's moral and ethical code, and the combination of these will determine one's outward behavior. Those who live according to their moral and ethical code we often refer to as having integrity.

We all know a Plain Jane and Fancy Flossy, Chatty Cathy and Mousy Mary. What makes us give them these titles? We give them these titles because of the way they dress, talk, and conduct themselves around us. The woman who wants to have a role of leadership must be concerned about both her outward and inward appearance and learn to cultivate both.

Outward Appearance
1 Timothy 2:9–10

9 In like manner also, that women adorn themselves in modest apparel, with shamefacedness and sobriety; not with broided hair, or gold, or pearls, or costly array;

10 But (which becometh women professing godliness) with good works.

1 Peter 3:3–4

3 Whose adorning let it not be that outward adorning of plaiting the hair, and of wearing of gold, or of putting on of apparel;

4 But let it be the hidden man of the heart, in that which is not corruptible, even the ornament of a meek and quiet spirit, which is in the sight of God of great price.

Ladies, this does not mean we can't dress our best and wear fashionable clothes or pretty jewelry and have our hair fixed and apply makeup. These verses simply mean that our appearance should not be showy, worldly, or flashy. We do not need to wear dresses down to our ankles and necklines up to our chins, nor do we have to be plain and ordinary. We, as Christian ladies, can and should (as much as our budget allows us) strive to be dressed fashionably and not look like yesterday's news. We, especially the older we get, need to dress in age-appropriate clothing, hair, and makeup. Remember that we are trying to show the world the hope that lies within us, and it is not the hope of eternal youth but of having Christ in us, the hope of glory. When it comes to our appearance, modesty is the key, especially for those in leadership. We need to remember we are to look God-like, not odd-like.

Two other things we learn from these verses that add to our reputation are good works and a meek and quiet spirit. The Lord will always use people who have proven themselves through good works. No task, no matter how insignificant you may think it is, goes unnoticed by the Lord. The best place for women to begin doing good works for the Lord is in their homes. Having a meek and quiet spirit is important, both in the home and outside the home. We do not have to look any further for a reason we should cultivate a meek and quiet spirit than the end of the verse, which says that our efforts will be "in the sight of God of great price."

Inward Appearance

1 Timothy 3:11

Even so must their wives be grave, not slanderers, sober, faithful in all things.

Terms Defined:

Grave: dignified and worthy of respect

Not slanderers: not damaging others' reputations

Sober: having self-control and a sound mind as well as common sense

Faithful: dependable in all matters

Titus 2:3

The aged women likewise, that they be in behaviour as becometh holiness, not false accusers, not given to much wine, teachers of good things.

Terms Defined:

Behaviour as becometh holiness: her conversations, gestures, and habits are holy in manner and action

Not false accusers: she does not participate in slander or gossip

Not given to much wine: she is not under the control of any addictive substance nor involved in addictive practices of any kind

Teaches good things: both by her words through teaching and her conduct and actions

A woman does not become a Titus 2 woman overnight. No, this behavior in holiness is acquired through discipline and conforming to His image by spending time in His Word in prayer and by applying what we have learned. Godly behavior is real and seen in everyday situations by how we act and react to those situations. Holiness is from the inside out and is seen all the time, not just at church or around church people. If you want to know how godly someone is, just ask his or her family.

A woman who is godly has a genuine love for the Lord, and her life speaks that loud and clear. She does not have to tell others about her holiness. Her life is a living testimony of her faith and godliness. It was no coincidence that Paul told Titus that the first thing women should be is holy, for we cannot bring anyone closer to the Lord than we are ourselves. Let me repeat that: we cannot bring anyone closer to the Lord than we are ourselves. Many people can fake piety, but holiness is from the inside, and it is often revealed through our words! It is not an accident that false accusers are listed next.

The word for slanderers and false accusers in the original language of the Bible is *diabolos*. This word means false accuser, devil, and slanderer. This is an interesting word, for it is found 36 times in the New Testament; and 33 times, it is referring to the devil. In the remaining three verses, it is referring to people, and two of these three verses are referring to women (1 Timothy 3:11, 2 Timothy 3:3, Titus 2:3)! A godly woman's mouth will have words of wisdom and have a tongue that is kind. She will not be a slanderer (damage another's reputation), backbiter, talebearer, or one who causes strife. The Bible has much to say about our speech and what comes out of our mouths. James, Psalms 34:12–13, and Proverbs 32:26 are just a few places to look.

Holy women are also not given to much wine; they do not allow any addictive behavior to control them. We often think of alcohol, cigarettes, and drugs when we think of addictive behaviors, but there are other things that we can become addicted to in this life. Romance novels, TV programs, physical fitness, shopping, Facebook, Pinterest . . . OK, now I am meddling, but you get my point. All these things are OK as long as they do not dominate our lives, our speech, or our behavior.

The final point Paul makes here is that older women should be teachers of good things, meaning those who teach right things (right and true). One cannot teach something one has not learned. Don't you feel sorry for the student who sits before a teacher who does not know the subject he or she is teaching and is only one chapter ahead of the students? The best teachers are know the subject he or she is teaching and is only one chapter ahead of the students? The best teachers are the ones who have lived or experienced what they are teaching.

Teaching: Who, What, Why

Whom She Teaches

Whom are holy and godly women to teach? They are to teach younger women.

4 That they may teach the young women . . .

Notice the little word "that." In verse 3, Paul laid the foundation for what qualities a woman in leadership should have and tells us why she needs this foundation in verse 4—so that she may teach younger women. As a society, we have gotten away from the Lord's teachings, and our young ladies and many of our older ladies are being taught by Oprah, Dr. Phil, Lindsay Lohan, Miley Cyrus, and Lady Gaga (I am still trying to figure her out). May the Lord help us get back to the basics, in which the mothers, grandmothers, aunts, older sisters, and friends teach our young women how to be godly women. We need older women who are willing to mentor younger women. You may think you could never be a mentor. News alert! You are already a mentor. Someone is watching you and mimicking everything you do. Whether you realize it or not, you are teaching someone, you are being watched 24/7, and you are teaching by example every day.

We teach those things we have personally learned and experienced through our own Bible study and our walk with the Lord. As we teach younger women those good things, we must make sure that our talk matches our walk. It is so true that our actions will speak louder than our words. For example, teaching the meaning of the following verses will be effective only if the women we mentor see these spiritual truths lived out in our lives during times of uncertainties and when we come under trials:

Philippians 4:6–8

6 Be careful for nothing; but in every thing by prayer and supplication with thanksgiving let your requests be made known unto God.

7 And the peace of God, which passeth all understanding, shall keep your hearts and minds through Christ Jesus.

8 Finally, brethren, whatsoever things are true, whatsoever things are honest, whatsoever things are just, whatsoever things are pure, whatsoever things are lovely, whatsoever things are of good report; if there be any virtue, and if there be any praise, think on these things.

What good would it be to teach the meaning of these verses if others were to see us worried and anxious and having no peace when we are faced with trials? Do you think your teaching would help people if all they saw and heard from you was doom and gloom?

Galatians 5:22–23

22 But the fruit of the Spirit is love, joy, peace, long-suffering, gentleness, goodness, faith,

23 Meekness, temperance: against such there is no law.

Are we displaying the fruit of the Spirit in our lives before we try to teach it?

Note: A female does not have to be a Senior Saint to teach younger women. There are many godly teenage girls and college students who are living holy lives and are capable of taking younger girls under their wings to start instilling in them Biblical principles.

What She Teaches

Titus 2:4–5

4 . . . to <u>love</u> [Gk. *philandros*, to have affection for] their husbands, to <u>love</u> their children,

5 To be discreet, chaste, keepers at home, good, obedient to their own husbands

The next thing that Paul says needs to be taught to younger women I find amazing: to love their husbands, to love their children. We are to teach younger women to have the proper affection for their husbands. One would think that love would come naturally to women, especially love for their children, but apparently it needs to be taught.

While I was working on this point, the movie *Beauty and the Beast* came to my mind. Remember how Belle was kind and affectionate to the Beast? And that love did what? It broke the evil spell, her prince was revealed, and they lived happily ever after. Now that was a terrific Disney movie, but it is also a Biblical truth. Ephesians 4:32 says, "And be ye kind one to another, tenderhearted, forgiving one another, even as God for Christ's sake hath forgiven you."

I do believe this is what we are to teach young women in regard to their husbands. It is easy to forgive our girlfriends, parents, children, and friends for things they have done to upset or hurt us; but for some reason, to be kind, tenderhearted, and forgiving to our husbands is more difficult. We need to get back to following the Lord's will in ALL our relationships, especially those with our husbands. How often do we see women tolerate their husbands rather than enjoy and love them? They put them down instead of building them up. A sharp word instead of a kind word is spoken. I see some women who truly love and show more affection to their dogs than they do to their husbands.

In Biblical days, marriages were often arranged for political, economic, and social reasons. Many times, there was no romance before a marriage nor after, and one can understand why women were supposed to teach others to love their husbands. In today's society, one would think that love would be the first reason for marriage, but many of our young couples confuse lust with love. So many marriages start off on the wrong principles and are headed for doom before the first year is over.

Today, broken homes and absent dads are other factors in why a young woman would have to be taught to love her husband. There are no role models in many young women's lives today. Where are the Titus 2 women who are teaching these young girls how to love their husbands? To love their children . . . I am sure most of us are thinking that should be a natural love and should not have to be taught, but we live in a society that has devalued life. Abortion is the norm in our country today. Recently, a judge passed a law that states that females of any age can buy the morning-after pill, and we wonder why we need to teach women to love their children.

When I first read in Titus (over 40 years ago) that women are to be taught to love their children, I could not grasp the meaning of it. Motherhood, I thought, was as natural as putting butter on a biscuit. I was raised by a loving mother and just naturally learned how to be a mother through Mom, but not every young woman, especially today, has that privilege, and they really do not have a clue about how to love their children.

These women need to be taught how to love their children with proper care and loving discipline. They need to be taught how to be their children's mothers, not their BFFs. A child will have many BFFs in his or her lifetime, but a mother is not one of them. Trust me: that day will come, and it will be here faster than you think. One day, you are sending them to school with their lunch. And the next day, they are picking you up for lunch, and you have become your child's BFF.

What else are mothers to be taught, according to verse 5?

5 To be discreet, chaste, keepers at home, good, obedient to their own husbands.

Terms Defined:

Discreet: prudent, judicious, and cautious.

Chaste: clean, pure in heart and life, and modest.

Keepers at home: means not neglecting your family and home duties. This is not against women working outside the home. Our economy today makes it necessary for many women to work outside the home, and my hat is off to all of you who do so and still manage to be keepers of the home. God bless you! This simply means her home (house and family) is not neglected. She is interested in and attentive to home duties (cooking, cleaning, laundry, etc.).

Good: she is kind, benevolent, and charitable.

Obedient to her own husband: means just what it says. Her husband is the person she listens to and follows (remember that submission thing, ladies).

Why She Teaches

5 . . . that the word of God be not blasphemed.

146

These women need to teach the younger women these things so that, when they profess to know the Lord, no evil can be spoken of or about them that would bring reproach to the gospel because of their behavior and actions.

Conclusion

When I think of Titus 2 women who have all these qualities, I am reminded of two ladies: Granny Smith and Ruth Chappell from Tabernacle in Greenville, South Carolina. These women walked, talked, and lived for the Lord daily and were willing to teach younger women. They taught by their lives in action.

Ruth Chappell was a quiet woman who loved her Lord and Savior, Jesus Christ, and wanted nothing more than to serve Him. She would write to me faithfully while I was in Austria. She said something to me in one of her letters that I will never forget.

She mentioned that, every time she would give her missions offering, she would pray, "Lord bless Preacher Dave, 'Putter', and all their little jewels (our kids)." While home on furlough, we visited her in her home. It was by far the humblest house I had ever been in; however, it was a home rich in those things money cannot buy—a home rich in love for the Lord, the Bible, and His people—and that love bounced off of every wall. She had her priorities straight. She loved her Lord and lived a humble, modest life to give what little money she had to further the gospel to others. Ruth taught me so much about priorities, love, humility, and giving, and she never said a word; she just lived by example.

When we met Granny Smith, she was close to 80 years old. She had been widowed at 35 and left with two young children. A beautiful lady both inside and out, she was like a magnet: she could draw people to her, especially young people, just by smiling. Many times, I would watch her go to the altar and pray to be a better witness for the Lord. She was an amazing woman. I asked her why she never remarried. I will never forget what she said. She looked at me with a smile on her face and said, "Well, at first, I could not find a man who was as good as my husband was, and then as time went on, I realized I would never find a man who could take better care of me than Jesus!"

This little poem was what Granny Smith lived by:
Yesterday He helped me,
Today He did the same.
How long will this continue?
FOREVER, Praise His name!

These two godly ladies had all the qualities that a woman in leadership needs; however, they did not hold positions of leadership within the church, but they were effective leaders of many younger women. This brings us to our final thought: leadership doesn't need a title, position, or classroom. It just requires someone to lead.

149

Men in Ministry

There is a very interesting beginning to men in ministry. If you look for words like "priest," "prophet," and "preacher" in your app's search feature, it will lead you to people and places where it all began. Here's the beginning. In the Garden of Eden, the Lord walked in the midst of it with Adam and Eve. Before the fall of man, God Himself was all that man needed to know to understand His will. They just talked about things. It wasn't until after man sinned that the Lord had to make other provisions to guide Adam spiritually. The first mention of a **priest** is found in Genesis 14:18: "And Melchizedek king of Salem brought forth bread and wine: and he was the <u>priest</u> of the most high God." This rather mysterious person is described much later in the New Testament as a type of the Lord Jesus Christ Himself. It has always been God who has had the greatest concern and love for the creatures that He created in His own image and likeness. That still stands today.

The word "**prophet**" is first mentioned in a dream that God gave to King Abimelech. Abraham told the king that Sarah was his sister, and so the king decided to take her to be his wife. The Lord intervened in a dream and gave Abimelech this warning in Genesis 20:7: "Now therefore restore the man [Abraham] his wife; for he is a prophet, and he shall pray for thee, and thou shalt live: and if thou restore her not, know thou that thou shalt surely die, thou, and all that are thine."

Solomon is the first person to be called a **preacher** in Ecclesiastes. In my German Bible, there isn't any book named Ecclesiastes; it is called *Prediger*, which translates to "preacher." The first mention of "preacher" begins here, in Ecclesiastes 1:1: "The words of the Preacher, the son of David, king in Jerusalem."

"**Pastor**" is found only once in its singular form in both the Old and the New Testament. The plural,

151

"pastors," is found seven times and used only once in a positive context. The first use of "pastors" begins here, in Jeremiah 2:8: "The priests said not, Where is the LORD? and they that handle the law knew me not: the <u>pastors</u> also transgressed against me, and the prophets prophesied by Baal, and walked after things that do not profit."

In the New Testament, "pastor" is closely linked to two other words: "bishop" (overseer) and "elder" (a term of rank or office). The second office is that of deacon. This passage brings into view three of the four positions for men in ministry in the beginning of the New Testament's transitional period, which ended with the death of the apostles, as evidenced in Philippians 1:1: "Paul [an <u>apostle, a sent one</u>] and Timotheus [a pastor], the servants of Jesus Christ, to all the saints in Christ Jesus which are at Philippi, with the bishops and <u>deacons</u>." To see the rest of these positions, we reflect on Ephesians 4:10–11: 10 "He [Christ] that descended is the same also that

152

ascended up far above all heavens, that he might fill all things." 11 "And he gave some, apostles; and some, prophets; and some, evangelists; and some pastors and teachers [The pastor is literally the teacher.]."

You may be wondering at this point about missionaries: where do they fit in the picture? Missionaries actually fit into the category of apostles. The word "apostle" means a sent one. There are two groups of apostles—apostles of Christ and apostles of the church. Apostles of Christ had to have seen Christ after His resurrection and have been called and sent by Him. The Apostle Paul saw Christ after His resurrection, on the road to Damascus and is included in the first group of apostles. He was also the first to be sent out under the authority of a local church. Here are the verses that put this in context. Acts 13:1–4: 1 "Now there were in the church that was at Antioch certain prophets and teachers; as Barnabas, and Simeon that was called Niger, and Lucius of Cyrene, and Manaen, which had been brought up with Herod the tetrarch, and Saul." 2 "As they ministered to the Lord, and fasted, <u>the Holy Ghost said, Separate me Barnabas and Saul for the work whereunto I have called them</u>." 3 "And when they had fasted and prayed, <u>and laid their hands on them, they sent them away</u>." 4 "<u>So they, being sent forth</u> by the Holy Ghost, departed unto Seleucia; and from thence they sailed to Cyprus." 5 "And when they were at Salamis, they preached the word of God in the synagogues of the Jews: and they had also John to their minister."

Missionaries are called by God and sent out by local churches to preach the Word of God and establish autonomous, indigenous churches. There are also ministries to help missionaries achieve this goal. Some examples would be other supporting churches, mission boards, printing ministries, construction teams, medical teams, and many more. <u>The true missionary</u> is one who leaves his job, home, family,

and country with the idea of never coming back—
except for the required furloughs and medical needs.

Evangelists are itinerant preachers of the gospel who
go from person to person or place to place as they are
led by the Holy Spirit. Perhaps the best example is
found in Acts 8:26–29: 26 "And the angel of the Lord
spake unto Philip, saying, Arise, and go toward the
south unto the way that goeth down from Jerusalem
unto Gaza, which is desert." 27 "And he arose and
went: and, behold, a man of Ethiopia, an eunuch of
great authority under Candace queen of the
Ethiopians, who had the charge of all her treasure, and
had come to Jerusalem for to worship," 28 "Was
returning, and sitting in his chariot read Esaias the
prophet." 29 "Then the Spirit said unto Philip, Go
near, and join thyself to this chariot." Evangelists,
pastors, deacons, and missionaries all have an
awesome responsibility to be men of God.

The pastoral epistles give the requirements that God expects candidates to have to fill these positions of service. When people who have been called by the Holy Spirit and directed by Him are ordained into the appropriate ministries, they will be able to accomplish the Lord's will by His divine providence.

A job description forms the basis of what is expected of the person seeking to fill a specific position. What you are about to memorize is what God expects of His servants. On one occasion, the Lord said to His disciples, in John 13:17: "If ye know these things, happy are ye if ye do them." This is a fitting application of the 16 musts that surround the lives of those chosen for ministry. The need to memorize these musts is obvious. Or at least it should be! Memorizing your job requirements gives both you and your boss a clear view of job objectives and clarifies your responsibilities. If you are a man in ministry and you have never memorized these points, how could you be happy doing them? You need to look at these musts because a must is not an option.

Lesson 9 Memorization for Women

What are the qualities of women in leadership? Please write them from memory and give a brief explanation for each point.

1. Her submission

2. Her character

3. Her outward appearance

4. Her inward appearance

5. Her teachings: who, what, and why

Lesson 9 Memorization for Men

Please write or say from memory the 10 musts and the six must-nots along with their meanings.

QUALIFICATIONS (16) OF A NEW TESTAMENT PASTOR—1 TIMOTHY 3—10 MUSTS AND 6 MUST-NOTS

10 MUSTS WITH A DEFINITION OF TERMS

He must be:

1. Apt to Teach = able to make people learn
2. Blameless = unchargeable
3. Given to Hospitality = lover of hospitality
4. Of Good Behavior = mannerly and polite
5. Of Good Report = of those from without
6. The Husband of One Wife = not divorced and remarried
7. Patient = able to persevere during trials
8. Able to Rule Well = his own family first
9. Sober = a wise decision maker

10. Vigilant = on guard against sin

6 MUST-NOTS WITH A DEFINITION OF TERMS

He must not be:

1. A Brawler = not argumentative
2. Covetous = not envious of others
3. Given to Wine = not given to alcohol
4. Greedy = not just in it for the money
5. A Novice = not responding to the flesh
6. A Striker = not apt to use his fist

LESSON 10: HERMENEUTICS 101

. . . *Sir, we would see Jesus.* Yes, you will find Him in hermeneutics, for Jesus used a number of the hermeneutical rules in refuting the devil in Matthew chapter four.

This question has been asked many times: "Why are there so many different beliefs and denominations?" Someone wisely answered, "Because not everyone who believes in God and reads the Bible has the same **rules** for interpreting it." The rules that determine how any piece of literature is interpreted are collectively called "hermeneutics." It can be defined as the branch of knowledge that deals with interpretation, especially of the Bible or literary texts. Without the application of these rules, "anything goes." This simply means that, without the proper understanding and application of the basic hermeneutical principles, a person can distort any passage of Scripture and give it a meaning that is foreign to the writer's intent. To see how Jesus used one of the rules of hermeneutics to correct the Devil's misinterpretation of a verse, read the following:

Matthew 4:5–7

5 Then the devil taketh him up into the holy city, and setteth him on a pinnacle of the temple,

6 And saith unto him, If thou be the Son of God, cast thyself down: for it is written, He shall give his angels charge concerning thee: and in their hands they shall bear thee up, lest at any time thou dash thy foot against a stone.

7 <u>Jesus said unto him, It is written again, Thou shalt not tempt the Lord thy God.</u>

The interpretation of a verse or any portion of Scripture can be tested hermeneutically to determine whether it is right or wrong, true or false. It doesn't matter how "lettered" the commentator may be. Because we live in a generation that has basically no ingrained knowledge of the rules of hermeneutics, people project in preaching and teaching what they find agreeable to them in their favorite commentaries.

Of the eight basic rules or principles of hermeneutics, these three are the most important. They are listed in order of significance: the context rule, the harmony rule, and the grammar rule. The "golden rule" of Bible interpretation has its application in the first of these three: "If the plain sense makes common sense, seek no other sense." This simply means to take it literally unless there is an indicator that would lead in some other direction (e.g., a figure of speech or a symbol).

Hermeneutical principles are the rules that govern how any written text is to be understood. When applied to Scripture, these rules preserve the authority of God's Word and expose the errors of those who may not know them and apply them.

Here is the list of the eight rules. Get to know and recognize them well as you read Scripture. They will become your best friends and enable you to *rightly divide the word of truth.*

1. Context Principle - The applicable meaning of a word, phrase, sentence, paragraph, chapter, or book of the Bible is taken from the circumstances and conditions that surround it. For example, in John 10:30, why did Jesus say that He and the Father are one? The context rule is the most important rule because it forces the reader to examine the overall thought by what is said before and after the thought is expressed. The meaning of a passage in Scripture must be interpreted in this manner so the reader will know the intent of the writer.

2. Harmony Principle - A truth that is God-given will always be in harmony with the whole of God's Word. For example, consider Genesis 3:21: "Unto Adam also and to his wife did the LORD God make coats of

skins, and clothed them." The harmony rule is the second most important rule because it highlights all contradictions to any previous truth that has been established.

3. Grammar Principle - Every verse of Scripture must be interpreted in agreement with or in terms of its grammatical structure. The grammar rule is the third most important rule because it determines, controls, and limits the interpretation syntactically. Syntax is the branch of linguistics that deals with the application of set rules in a language.

4. Language Principle - This is the awareness of how language is being used in the verse (i.e., literal, figurative, or symbolic language and the grammatical functions that apply to each part of speech). In John 8:58, Jesus said, "Before Abraham was, I am." In John 10:9, he says, "I am the door . . . ." And in Revelation 8:6, we read, "And the seven angels which

had the seven trumpets prepared themselves to sound." The trumpet is a symbol for judgment.

5. Double Reference Principle - This refers to a statement that has more than one application or way of being fulfilled (e.g., Psalms 22:1: "My God, my God, why hast thou forsaken me?"; And Matthew 27:46: "And about the ninth hour Jesus cried with a loud voice, saying, My God, my God, why hast thou forsaken me?").

6. First Reference Principle - Sets forth a truth from its first usage that is consistent throughout the whole Bible (e.g., Genesis 2:17: "But of the tree of the knowledge of good and evil, thou shalt not eat of it: for in the day that thou eatest thereof thou shalt surely die.").

7. Progressive Revelation Principle - This principle concerns a truth that requires additional information to make it clear (e.g., Genesis 3:15: "And I will put

enmity between thee and the woman, and between thy seed and her seed; it shall bruise thy head, and thou shalt bruise his heel"; Isaiah 7:14 and 9:6; Matthew 1:21; Revelation 1:7–8).

8. Main Revelation Principle - This is a book, chapter, or verse in which a certain truth is fully revealed. Some examples include 1 Corinthians 15, The Resurrection, verse 4: "he [Jesus Christ] rose again the third day."

1 Corinthians 15:12: "Now if Christ be preached that he rose from the dead, how say some among you that there is no resurrection of the dead?"

1 Corinthians 15:17: "And if Christ be not raised, your faith is vain; ye are yet in your sins."

1 Corinthians 15:35–36: "But some man will say, How are the dead raised up? and with what body do they come?" 36 "Thou fool, that which thou sowest is not quickened, except it die."

1 Corinthians 15:50–53: "Now this I say, brethren, that flesh and blood cannot inherit the kingdom of God; neither doth corruption inherit incorruption." 51 "Behold, I show you a mystery; We shall not all sleep, but we shall all be changed," 52 "In a moment, in the twinkling of an eye, at the last trump: for the trumpet shall sound, and the dead shall be raised incorruptible, and we shall be changed." 53 "For this corruptible must put on incorruption, and this mortal must put on immortality."

The Most Common Hermeneutical Errors

Rightly dividing (to cut straight or expound correctly) the Word of Truth requires the knowledge and application of hermeneutical principles. When these principles are not followed, many varied interpretations of the same verse will result. One of the least understood and perhaps most abused aspects of Biblical explanation is interpreting the Bible grammatically. One cannot interpret a verse in a way that is contrary to its grammatical structure. Many good men have stumbled on this point.

Let's consider just four simple aspects of grammatical interpretation: time; gender; pronoun/antecedent agreement; and out of necessity, context. The following examples illustrate some of the most common hermeneutical errors.

Proverbs 29:18

Often, just the first half of this verse is quoted, and frequently an application principle violation (an application that changes the meaning of the verse) is made. "Where there is no vision [open revelation from God], the people perish [cast off restraint]: but he that keepeth the law, happy is he."

Psalms 12:5–7

Gender and pronoun agreement violation: often, verses 6 and 7 are quoted without verse 5, which

169

contains the antecedent for the pronoun "them" in verse 7.

5 For the oppression of the poor, for the sighing of the needy, now will I arise, saith the LORD; I will set him in safety from him that puffeth at him.

6 The words of the LORD are pure words: as silver tried in a furnace of earth, purified seven times.

7 Thou shalt keep them, O LORD, thou shalt preserve them from this generation for ever.

The antecedent for "them" in verse 7 is found in verse 5, and it is the poor and the needy.

Charles Rice—an independent, fundamental Baptist pastor who has studied both Greek and Hebrew—had these comments about verse 7: "I agree with the commentaries. The term 'words' is a feminine noun. The 'them' of verse 7 is masculine. I conclude by this and the context that the 'them' refers to the poor of verse 5."

Matthew Henry's Commentary, Vol. 3, p. 281, Psalms 12:7: "He will keep them (the poor and needy, His people) from this generation. From being debauched by them and drawn away from God, from mingling with them and learning their works. In times of general apostasy, the Lord knows those that are His, and they shall be enabled to keep their integrity."

C. H. Spurgeon, *Treasury of David*, Vol. 1, p. 143, verse 7: "To fall into the hands of an evil generation, so as to be baited by their cruelty, or polluted by their influence, is an evil to be dreaded beyond measure; but it is an evil foreseen and provided for in the text. In life many a saint has lived a hundred years before his age, as though he had darted his soul into the brighter future, and escaped the mists of the beclouded present: he has gone to his grave unreverenced and misunderstood, and lo! as generations come and go, upon a sudden the hero is unearthed, and lives in the admiration and love of the excellent of the earth; preserved for ever from the generation which stigmatized him as a sower of sedition, or burned him as a heretic. It should be our daily prayer that we may rise above our age as the mountaintops above the clouds, and may stand out as a heaven-pointing pinnacle high above the mists of ignorance and sin which roll around us. O Eternal Spirit, fulfil in us the faithful saying of this verse! Our faith believes those two assuring words, and cries, Thou shalt, thou shalt."

John Gill, online Bible commentator, verse 7: "Thou shall keep them, O Lord. Not the words before mentioned, as Aben Ezra explains it, for the affix is masculine and not feminine; not but God has wonderfully kept and preserved the sacred writings; and He keeps every word of promise which He has made; and the doctrines of the Gospel will always continue from one generation to another; but the sense is that God will keep the poor and needy, and such as He sets in safety, as Kimchi rightly observes: they are not their own keepers, but God is the keeper of them;

he keeps them by His power, and in His Son, in whose hands they are, and who is able to keep them from falling; they are kept by Him from a total and final falling away; from the dominion and damning power of sin, and from being devoured by Satan, and from the evil of the world: and this the psalmist had good reason to believe, because of the love of God to them, His covenant with them, and the promises of safety and salvation He has made unto them. . . ."

Ephesians 2:8

Often, grace—or faith—is said to be "the gift of God" in this verse, but the genders do not agree with this rendering.

"For by grace are ye saved through faith; and that [or this (salvation) is] not of yourselves: it [our salvation] is the gift of God."

Note: Either "that" or "this" could be used in the verse above. Both are used as demonstrative pronouns to refer to a thought expressed earlier. In our example, it is referring to verse 4.

The relative "that," which is in the neuter gender, cannot stand for faith or grace, which are feminine. The antecedent for "that" and "it" must match in gender.

Ephesians 4:11

Hermeneutical Principle of Grammar = One cannot interpret the content of anyone's writings (especially the Word of God) contrary to its grammatical construction. Rightly dividing (to cut straight or expound correctly) the Word of Truth requires applying this hermeneutical principle to be consistent with the rules of grammar that govern each reader's exposition of a text regardless of one's feelings or opinions.

The verse in question is Ephesians 4:11: "And he gave some, apostles; and some, prophets; and some, evangelists; and some, pastors and teachers;"

11 "And <kai> he gave some, apostles; and <de> some, prophets; and <de> some, evangelists; and <de> some, pastors and <kai> teachers."

Point of Controversy: Is the pastor also the teacher, or is being a teacher a different office or calling that is being introduced in this verse? How can one know the answer to this question?

There is a rule in Greek syntax that is connected to the presence and absence of the article. It is called Granville Sharp's Rule. It is as follows:

When the copulative "kai" connects two nouns of the same case, if the article "ho" (I have to spell the definite article in English phonetics) or any of its cases precedes the first of the said nouns or participles and is not repeated before the second noun or participle, then the latter always relates to the same person expressed or described by the first noun or participle—denoted by or described by the first named person. In other words, when two nouns in the same case are connected by the kai and the first noun is articular and the second is anarthrous, then the second noun refers to the same person or thing to which the first noun refers and is a further description of it.

Kenneth S. Wuest, *THE PRACTICAL USE OF THE GREEK NEW TESTAMENT,* p. 22, par. 1:
Some pron. = "an indefinite or unspecified number or portion: We took some of the books to the auction." This was quoted from the *American Heritage Dictionary.*

Kenneth Wuest's comments on Ephesians 4:11 are: "The word 'pastor' is poimen, 'a shepherd.' The words 'pastors' and 'teachers' are in a construction called Granville Sharp's Rule, which indicates that they refer to one individual. The one who shepherds God's flock is also a teacher of the Word, having both the gifts of shepherding and teaching the flock. God's ideal pastor is one who engages in a didactic ministry, feeding the saints on expository preaching, giving them the rich food of the Word." Page 101, *Ephesians and Colossians, in the Greek New Testament.*

We have both the giving of the rule in the *Practical Use of the Greek New Testament* and the application of the rule in the author's commentary on the Book of Ephesians. So based on the rules of Greek syntax, one can rightly say that, hermeneutically, Ephesians 4:11 is saying, "Pastors even teachers, For the perfecting of the saints, for the work of the ministry, for the edifying of the body of Christ."

John 20:17

Verb parsing must be a part of the exposition.

"Jesus saith unto her, Touch me not; for I am not yet ascended to my Father: but go to my brethren, and say unto them, I ascend unto my Father, and your Father; and to my God, and your God."

Nelson #135, Study Bible Notes on John 20:17:
"Touch me not" is a present imperative, forbidding
the continuation of an action already begun. "Stop
clinging to me" is a helpful paraphrase.

Adam Clark, Commentary on John 20:17:
"'Touch me not,' 'Cling not to me,' has this sense in
Job 31:7, where the Septuagint uses it for the Hebrew,
which signifies to cleave, cling, stick, or be glued to.
From Matt. 28:9, it appears that some of the women
held him by the feet and worshiped him. Matt. 28:9:
'And as they [the women] went to tell his disciples,
behold, Jesus met them, saying, All hail. And they
came and held him by the feet, [just moments later
after leaving Mary this took place] and worshiped
him.' This probably Mary did also; and our Lord
seems to have spoken to her to this effect: 'Spend no
longer time with me now: I am not going immediately
to heaven—you will have several opportunities of
seeing me again: but go and tell my disciples, that I
am, by and by, to ascend to my Father and God, who

178

is your Father and God also. Therefore, let them take courage.'"

Lesson 10 Memorization

Please list the eight principles from memory and give one example of their application in Scripture. Say or write the chapter and verse reference, and give a brief description of how each is used.

Question 1: Which three of the eight rules are the most important and why?

Context

Harmony

Grammar

Question 2: What is the golden rule of Bible interpretation? Write or say your answer!

"If the plain sense makes common sense, seek no other sense." This simply means to take any text literally unless otherwise indicated.

LESSON 11: FIGURES OF SPEECH

. . . Sir, we would see Jesus. Yes, you will find Him in figures of speech, for Jesus is described with beautiful word portraits of splendor and glory.

One of the most important things to remember about figures of speech I learned when witnessing to a Jehovah's Witness (JW). We were talking about Luke 16:19–31. The Lord Jesus gave a description of what happened to two people after they died. One was saved, and the other was lost. The saved man (Lazarus, the beggar) was in paradise, and the lost man (the rich man) was in hell. The JW expressed his objection to the reality of their experience by saying, "This is not literal; it's a parable." If this were to happen to you, you might reply with this question: "What is a parable?" A parable is a figure of speech. So now we come to the great importance of knowing exactly what a figure of speech is. <u>A figure of speech is a way of poetically expressing a literal truth</u>. Wow!

So what's the literal truth expressed by the Lord Jesus Christ in this passage? The literal truth is that, after the rich man died, he was in a place of torment, and Lazarus was in a place of blessing and comfort. From this example, one can see the importance of this lesson.

Here is a list of 10 of the most common figures of speech used in Scripture. By learning them, you will become more skilled in correctly expounding God's Word.

allegory (ăl′ĭ-gôr′ē) *n.*

A literary, dramatic, or pictorial device in which characters and events stand for abstract ideas, principles, or forces so that the literal sense has or suggests a parallel, deeper symbolic sense. Ps. 80, Gal. 4, Isa. 5, and Matt. 12:43–45 are examples of allegories.

anthropomorphism (ăn'thrə-pə-môr'fĭz'əm) *n.*   A figure of speech that attributes human motivation, characteristics, or behavior to God. Ps. 91:4: "He shall cover thee with his <u>feathers</u>, and under his <u>wings</u> shalt thou trust: his truth *shall be thy* shield and buckler."

euphemism (yōō'fə-mĭz'əm) *n.*   The act or an example of substituting a mild, indirect, or vague term for one considered harsh, blunt, or offensive. Example: "asleep" in 1 Thess. 4:15

hyperbole (hī-pûr'bə-lē) *n.*   A figure of speech in which exaggeration is used for emphasis or effect, as in *I could sleep for a year* or *This book weighs a ton.* [Latin *hyperbolē*, from Greek *huperbolē*, excess, from *huperballein*, to exceed: *huper*, beyond; see HYPER- + *ballein*.]. Matt. 19:24: "And again I say unto you, It is easier for a <u>camel to go through the eye of a needle</u> than for a rich man to enter into the kingdom of God."

183

metaphor (mĕt′ə-fôr′, -fər) *n.* A figure of speech in which a word or phrase that ordinarily designates one thing is used to designate another, thus making an implicit comparison, as in *a sea of troubles* or *All the world's a stage* (Shakespeare). Also, connecters ("as" or "like") are not used. Isa. 40:6: ". . . All flesh <u>*is*</u> grass . . ."; Ps. 23:1: "<u>The LORD *is* my shepherd</u>"; Matt. 26:26: ". . . Take, eat; <u>this is my body</u>."

metonymy (mə-tŏn′ə-mē) *n.* A figure of speech in which one word or phrase is substituted for another with which it is closely associated, as hyssop for blood in Ps. 51:7: "Purge me with <u>hyssop</u>, and I shall be clean . . . ."

paradox(păr′ə-dŏks′) *n.* A seemingly contradictory statement that may nonetheless be true: *the paradox that standing is more tiring than walking.* 1 Tim. 5:6: "But she that <u>liveth</u> in pleasure <u>is dead</u> while she <u>liveth</u>." Matt.16:25: " For whosoever will <u>save his</u>

life shall lose it: and whosoever <u>will lose his life</u> for my sake shall find it."

personification (pər-sŏn′ə-fĭ-kā′shən) *n.* A figure of speech in which inanimate objects or abstractions are endowed with human qualities or are represented as possessing human form, as in *Hunger sat shivering on the road* or *Flowers danced about the lawn.* Ps. 85:10: "Mercy and truth are met together; righteousness and <u>peace have kissed</u> each other." James 1:15: "Then when <u>lust hath conceived</u>, it bringeth forth sin: and sin, when it is finished, bringeth forth death."

simile (sĭm′ə-lē) *n.* A figure of speech in which two essentially unlike things are compared, often in a phrase introduced by *like* or *as,* which are used as connectors, as in *How like the winter hath my absence been* or *So are you to my thoughts as food to life* (Shakespeare). Isa. 53:6: "All <u>we like sheep</u> have gone astray. . . ." Acts 2:2–3 "And suddenly there

185

came a sound from heaven <u>as of a rushing mighty wind</u>, and it filled all the house where they were sitting." 3 "And there appeared unto them cloven <u>tongues like as of fire</u> . . . ."

Note: A parable is an expanded simile. It uses physical circumstances to present a spiritual truth. A figure of speech is simply a poetic way of expressing a literal truth.

synecdoche (sĭ-nĕk′də-kē) *n.* A figure of speech in which a part is used to represent the whole (as in *hand* for *sailor*), the whole for a part (as in *the law* for *police officer*). Gen. 36:6: "And Esau took his wives, and his sons, and his daughters, and all <u>the persons of his house</u>." Here, the *persons of his house* are used (the soul = *nephesh*), which functions as a synecdoche. Gen. 42:38: "Then shall ye bring down my <u>gray hairs</u> with sorrow to the grave." The gray hairs stand in for Jacob himself in his old age.

Lesson 11 Memorization

Please list or say the 10 figures of speech from memory and give one Scripture reference as an example of how they are used figuratively in the Bible. One easy way to remember the list is to arrange the figures of speech alphabetically like this: aa eh mm pp ss.

aa = allegory, anthropomorphism

eh = euphemism, hyperbole

mm = metaphor, metonymy

pp = paradox, personification

ss = simile, synecdoche

LESSON 12: HOMILETICS 101

. . . Sir, we would see Jesus. Yes, you will find Him in homiletics, for Jesus is the greatest preacher that ever walked this planet. Yes, we see Jesus from the first verse in Genesis to the last verse in Revelation. Open your Bible to any page, and you will find Jesus there.

Sermon = a message from the Word of God

Seven Different Types of Sermon Deliveries

1. Biographical - a study of a person
2. Expository - preaching the Word by following the context and the points the author makes
3. Historical Incident - makes a study of an event
4. Inferential - follows the text more loosely than expository without deviating from the context
5. Personal Testimony - a Christ-centered testimony

6. Textual - same as expository but limited to one verse or even part of a verse

7. Topical - preaching about a subject without support of the context to link related doctrinal statements

Question: What is expository preaching, and how does it differ from other types of preaching?

Answer: To expound what God said by giving an account of the context is preaching the Word. The "golden text" and possibly the best example of a verse that has the basic components of expository preaching is found in this verse: Nehemiah 8:8: "So they [Nehemiah, Ezra, and the Levites] read in the book in the law of God distinctly, and gave the sense, and caused them to understand the reading." To take a subject that is different from the text is preaching about the Word. Preaching the Word preserves God's authority and the continuity of His message, whereas preaching about the Word may not.

When there is a lack of hermeneutical and exegetical (digging out, from the text itself, what the author was saying to his readers) skills, expository preaching is difficult, and it requires a great deal more preparation. Expository preaching leaves the hearer with an understanding of the text from the context.

Question: What is the main difference between an expository message and the more frequently used topical message?

Answer: An expository message allows the speaker to find and speak the mind of God, which is preaching the Word. A topical message gives the speaker an opportunity to say what is on his or her own mind about the Word. Although topical messages have an important place in doctrinal studies, they provide very little insight when compared to a verse-by-verse study of Scripture in its context.

Lesson 12 Memorization

Please list the seven types of sermon deliveries, and explain the advantages or disadvantages of each style. Please list the three types of sermon deliveries that are considered expository.

Question 1: What is the difference between preaching the Word and preaching about the Word?

Answer: To expound what God said from the context is preaching the Word.

Question 2: What is the difference between preaching and teaching?

Answer: Preaching is an appeal to one's heart—you are looking for conviction and surrender. Teaching is an appeal to one's intellect—you are looking to reach the permanent memory with certain portions of the content. If one is not aware of these differences, one will not know how to focus and direct one's message.

GLOSSARY

All terms or verses that are marked with an asterisk are to be committed to permanent memory. The list of words to be memorized with their meanings is at the end of the glossary.

Accountability = one's responsibility to retain, apply, incorporate, and teach the Word of God
2 Tim. 2:15: "Study to show thyself approved unto God, a workman that needeth not to be ashamed, rightly dividing [to cut straight or expound correctly] the word of truth."

Application = the most important part of a sermon No application, no spiritual growth, no fruit
James 1:22: "But be ye doers of the word, and not hearers only, deceiving your own selves."

Atonement = cover Animal blood atoned for or covered our sins until Calvary. After that, Christ's blood cleansed the believers from all sin (1 John 1:7–9); therefore, it may be inapt to say that Christ's blood atoned for (only covered) our sins.

See Lewis Sperry Shafer, *Systematic Theology* (Grand Rapids: Kregel Publications, 1997), vol. 7, pp. 25–27.

*Born-Again = to be born from above or born of God (to have a spiritual birth)

John 3:3: "Jesus answered and said unto him, Verily, verily, I say unto thee, Except a man be born again [be born of God], he cannot see the kingdom of God."

John 1:12: "But as many as received him, to them gave he power to become the sons [children] of God, *even* to them that believe on his name."

John 1:13: "Which were born, not of <u>blood</u>, nor of the will of the <u>flesh</u>, nor of the will of <u>man</u>, but of God."

Note: Nothing we did—all of God.

Cleanse = to make one free from sin, defilement, and guilt   This is the New Testament word that replaces the Old Testament word "atonement/atone," meaning to cover.

1 John 1:7b: "The blood of Jesus Christ his Son cleanseth us from all sin."

1 John 1:9: " If we confess our sins, he is faithful and just to forgive us *our* sins, and to cleanse us from all unrighteousness."

The blood of Christ washes and cleanses believers from all sin. It makes them whiter than snow. It's better than bleach!   It more than amazing: it's awesome!

Exegesis = arriving at the same destination as the author in thought and intent by an exhaustive study or analysis, especially of a text   [Greek *exēgēsis*, from *exēgeisthai*, to interpret: *ex-*, ex- + *hēgeisthai*, to lead; see sāg- below.]

[1]"Exegesis is the skill of 'digging out,' from the text itself, what the author was saying to his readers. It is in exegesis where the parsing of verbs takes place. The opposite of exegesis is eisegesis, which is the projection of your own feelings and ideas into the text."

*Faith = an act of the human heart that is generated by trust God has proven that He is trustworthy, so we should trust Him. The opposite of faith is unbelief. Unbelief is an act of the human heart that trusts in man rather than the Creator. This lack of faith in God is what has produced humanism and the theory of evolution.

Glorification = Christ's holiness exhibited in the resurrected children of God

---

[1] Dr. Robert Morey, *The Trinity* (Grand Rapids: World Publishing, 1996), p. 31.

1 John 3:2: "Beloved, now are we the sons of God, and it doth not yet appear what we shall be: but we know that, when he shall appear, we shall be like him; for we shall see him as he is."

Glory of Christ = this may be describing His honor and dignity when exalted to the right hand of God the Father
John 17:24: "Father, I will that they also, whom thou hast given me, be with me where I am; that they may behold my glory, which thou hast given me: for thou lovedst me before the foundation of the world."

Grace (saving grace) = being released from judgment—getting what we do not deserve There are five different kinds of grace mentioned in the Bible.

*Hermeneutics = it is the science of interpreting a written text It uses fixed grammatical and literary rules that govern anyone who is honestly seeking to understand what a writer is saying in a text, especially the Bible.

*Justification = the act of God whereby our legal standing in heaven (guilty) is changed and we are <u>declared righteous</u>

Rom. 3:20–28: "Therefore by the deeds of the law there shall no flesh be justified in his sight: for by the law *is* the knowledge of sin." 21 "But now the righteousness of God <u>without the law</u> is manifested, being witnessed by the law and the prophets;" 22 "Even the righteousness of God *which is* by faith of Jesus Christ unto all and upon all them that believe: for there is no difference:" 23 "For all have sinned, and come short of the glory of God;" 24 " Being justified freely by his grace through the redemption that is in Christ Jesus:" 25 "Whom God hath set forth *to be* a propitiation through faith in his blood, to declare his righteousness for the remission of sins that are past, through the forbearance of God;" 26 "To declare, *I say,* at this time his righteousness: that he might be just, and the justifier of him which believeth in Jesus." 27 "Where *is* boasting then? It is excluded. By what law? Of works? Nay: but by the law of faith." 28 "Therefore we conclude that a man is justified by faith without the deeds of the law."

Every Christian ought to know Romans 4:4–5 by heart.

*Rom. 4:4–5: "Now to him that worketh is the reward not reckoned of grace, but of debt." 5 "But to him that worketh not, but believeth on him that justifieth the ungodly, his faith is counted for righteousness."

Meekness = to yield and submit to God
Galatians 5:22–23: "But the fruit of the Spirit is love, joy, peace, longsuffering, gentleness, goodness, faith," 23 "Meekness, temperance: against such there is no law."

Mercy = God's loving kindness and the relief from suffering; not getting what we do deserve

Propitiation = to satisfy EXPIATION and PROPITIATION (Ex pee ay' shuhn; Proh pih tee ay' shuhn) are terms used by Christian theologians to define and explain the meaning of Christ's death on the cross as it relates to God and believers. Expiation emphasizes the removal of guilt through a payment of the penalty, while propitiation emphasizes the appeasement or averting of God's wrath and justice. Both words are related to reconciliation because it is through Christ's death on the cross for our sins that we are reconciled to a God of holy love (Rom. 5:9–11, 2 Cor. 5:18–21, Col. 1:19–23).

Rom. 3:25 "Whom God hath set forth to be a propitiation through faith in his blood, to declare his righteousness for the remission of sins that are past, through the forbearance of God."

1 John 2:2: "And he is the propitiation for our sins: and not for ours only, but also for the sins of the whole world."

*Quickened = made alive

Reconciliation = a change in the relationship (because our sins have been blotted out) between God and man This change is based on Christ's redemptive work and a personal faith in the person and finished work of the Lord Jesus Christ. 2 Cor. 5:18–19: "And all things are of God, who hath reconciled us to himself by Jesus Christ, and hath given to us the ministry of reconciliation;" 19 "To wit, that God was in Christ, reconciling the world unto himself, not imputing their trespasses unto them; and hath committed unto us the word of reconciliation."

*Redeemed = delivered and set free from the bondage of sin The Redeemer, Jesus Christ, has delivered believers from the enslavement of sin and paid the ransom with His precious blood.   His sacrifice at Calvary delivered us from sin and granted new freedom for all those who have trusted in Him as their personal Lord and Savior.

*Regeneration = to create anew
Titus 3:5: "Not by works of righteousness which we have done, but according to his mercy he saved us, by the washing of regeneration, and renewing of the Holy Ghost."

*Repentance = a feeling of regret or sorrow toward God because you have sinned by disobeying Him A change of attitude about sin and God. A change of mind or a turning from your sin to follow a life of righteousness. Once you are saved, you will sin less, but you will never be sinless, yet it is your sincere desire to be. And one day, that wish will become your reality in a new, glorified body.

Faith and repentance are like the two sides of the coin called salvation. One cannot be separated from the other and have true Biblical salvation. Since the early 1970s, a different (false) gospel has been preached that has only invited sinners to believe and not repent, claiming that repentance is merely turning from unbelief toward belief. This type of evangelism, or "soul winning," can also be called "easy-believeism."

*Sanctification = the process of spiritual growth accomplished by yielding to the Holy Spirit as He applies the Word of God in such a way that results in a change in lifestyle

John 17:17: "Sanctify them through thy truth: thy word is truth."

Note: Because wisdom is often linked to knowledge, truth, and understanding, those three terms appear here together.

Knowledge = that which you know—it comes from learning. See Prov. 1:2.

Truth = that which conforms to reality, or conformity to fact or actuality; it comes from seeking.

Understanding = the proper application of <u>wisdom</u> to everyday situations. Understanding is what you do with what you figure out; it comes from applying wisdom. See Col. 1:9.

*Wisdom = the capability to discern the true nature of a situation. Wisdom is what you do with what you figure out from what you know; it comes from thinking. See Prov. 1:2.

Glossary Memorization

Question: What are the eight key terms in the glossary? Please write or say the definitions of these key terms.

Born-Again = to be born from above or born of God (to have a spiritual birth)

Faith = an act of the human heart that is generated by trust

Justification = the act of God whereby our legal standing in heaven (guilty) is changed and we are declared righteous

Quickened = made alive

Redeemed = delivered and set free from the bondage of sin

Regeneration = to create anew

Repentance = a feeling of regret or sorrow toward God because you have sinned by disobeying Him A change of attitude about sin and God.   A change of mind or a turning from your sin to follow a path of righteousness.

Wisdom = the capability to discern the true nature of a situation Wisdom is what you do with what you figure out from what you know; it comes from thinking.

Bibliography

Morey, Robert. *The Trinity*. Grand Rapids: World Publishing, 1996.

Philips, John. *Bible Explorer's Guide*. Neptune: Loizeaux Brothers, 1987.

Weeks, Dave. *CHECKMATE for Mormons and Jehovah's Witnesses*. Dacula: Baptist World Cult Evangelism, 2013.

Wilkinson, Bruce H. *The 7 Laws of the Learner*. Sisters: Multonomah Press, 1992.

Index